# CRACKING
# SHAKESPEARE

# ABOUT THE AUTHOR

Kelly Hunter is an award winning actor, director and teacher. Over the last thirty years she has performed major roles at the RSC, National Theatre and English Touring Theatre. For the RSC she has played *Lola* in *The Blue Angel, Constance* in *King John, Hermione* in *The Winters Tale* and *Goneril* in *King Lear.* For English Touring Theatre she has played *Rosalind* in *As you Like it* (TMA Best Actress award) *Nora* in *the Dolls House* and *Mrs Alving* in *Ghosts.* She has also worked extensively in film, TV and radio.

Kelly is the Artistic Director of Flute Theatre. In 2014 she directed *The Tempest* for children with autism, a co-production for the RSC and Ohio State University. Her most recent production, *Hamlet, who's there?* performed at the Gdansk Shakespeare Festival in 2015.

She has directed numerous productions of Shakespeare for UK and US students including *The Tempest*, *King Lear*, *A Midsummer Nights Dream, Cymbeline* and *Macbeth* for BADA. For RADA she has directed *Twelfth Night*, and at the Royal Central School of Speech and Drama she directed *Macbeth* and *Hamlet.* She has also directed an all female production of *Hamlet* at Mount view academy of Theatre Arts.

She is the author of *Shakespeare's Heartbeat; Drama Games for Children with Autism* and is the creator of the Hunter Heartbeat Method, a series of sensory games using Shakespeare for children with autism. This work is the basis of a longitudinal study at Ohio State University. She is a longstanding teacher of Shakespeare at the Actors Centre in London, working there since 2002.

# CRACKING SHAKESPEARE

## A Hands-on Guide for Actors and Directors + Video

## KELLY HUNTER

Bloomsbury Methuen Drama
An imprint of Bloomsbury Publishing Plc

B L O O M S B U R Y
LONDON · OXFORD · NEW YORK · NEW DELHI · SYDNEY

**Bloomsbury Methuen Drama**

An imprint of Bloomsbury Publishing Plc

| 50 Bedford Square | 1385 Broadway |
| London | New York |
| WC1B 3DP | NY 10018 |
| UK | USA |

**www.bloomsbury.com**

**Bloomsbury is a registered trademark of Bloomsbury Publishing Plc**

First published 2015

Copyright © Kelly Hunter 2015

**British Library Cataloguing-in-Publication Data**
A catalogue record for this book is available from the British Library.

ISBN: HB: 978-1-4725-2248-1
PB: 978-1-4725-3283-1
ePDF: 978-1-4725-2385-3
ePUB: 978-1-4725-3378-4

**Library of Congress Cataloging-in-Publication Data**
Hunter, Kelly, 1961-
Cracking Shakespeare : a hands-on guide for actors and directors + video / by Kelly Hunter.
pages cm
Includes bibliographical references and index.
ISBN 978-1-4725-2248-1 (hardback)– ISBN 978-1-4725-3283-1 (pbk.) 1. Shakespeare, William, 1564-1616–Dramatic production–Methodology. 2. Acting.
I. Title.
PR3091.H85 2015
792.9'5–dc23
2015014277

Typeset by Fakenham Prepress Solutions, Fakenham, Norfolk NR21 8NN
Printed and bound in India

Prove true, imagination, O, prove true

*Twelfth Night*, 3.4

# CONTENTS

# ACKNOWLEDGEMENTS

This book is dedicated to the students I directed in *The Tempest* (2007), *King Lear* (2008), *A Midsummer Night's Dream* (2011), *Cymbeline* (2012) and *Macbeth* (2015) at the BADA London Theatre Program and the Wilde group at BADA's Midsummer in Oxford Program, 2008.

With love to Jordan, Josh, Taron, Graeme, Charlie, Alex, Imi, Ailsa and Rosie, who I directed in *Twelfth Night* in 2011 at RADA.

Thanks to Ian Wooldridge who gave me the chance to begin directing productions of Shakespeare.

For the video filming: many thanks to Wendy Gadian and the Royal Central School of Speech and Drama; Ed Kemp and Lucy Skilbeck at RADA; Tom Wright (DOP); David Wigram, Chris Stone, Rob Thomas and Francis Sylver; and the students: Thomas Babbage, Tia Bannon, Ruby Campbell, Natasha Culley, Aaron Davies, Ryan Heenan, Tamara Lawrance, Alec Poore and Jessica Smith.

# INTRODUCTION

- How do I make Shakespeare's language mine?
- What does the iambic rhythm mean and how do I use it?
- What should I do when I first look at his words?
- When do I breathe?
- How do I stop myself doing a 'Shakespeare voice'?
  [https://vimeo.com/121688079]

These are the kind of questions I'm asked again and again when I start teaching or directing a new group of students. I have spent over ten years defining the best ways to reveal the answers, drawing upon my experience of performing major Shakespearean roles so that students and actors may genuinely take ownership of Shakespeare's language. This book contains the games, techniques and exercises I have created during my productions and workshops with actors, students and young people around the world.

Understanding the rhythm, sound, structure, keywords and rhetoric of Shakespeare's blank verse is essential; there's no getting round it. In Parts One and Two of this book, each chapter takes a particular element of verse speaking and introduces techniques and exercises that you can practise alone or in a group. These teach you how to recognize Shakespeare's patterns of language, within which lie unique acting clues and psychological insights. As the book progresses, it will become clear how these elements of verse speaking are inextricably linked and your confidence will grow as you find yourself identifying the patterns and thereby taking possession of the plays for yourself.

As much as possible, I demystify the 'rules' of verse speaking, teaching them clearly and frankly, demonstrating how they always relate to human experience and can be used by the actor or director to bring a character to life. Acting requires a constant balance of technique and feeling, and the particular challenge of performing Shakespeare lies in striking the balance between intellectual clarity and emotional soulfulness. An excess of technique will render you boring, whilst an excess of feeling may render you incomprehensible. The fundamental aim of the exercises is to allow you to capture the dynamic movement of thought from mind to mouth, as if you are speaking your thoughts for the very first time, embedded within which are your feelings.

It is equally essential, both for actors and directors, to fall in love with Shakespeare's words and forge their own connection to them. To that end the final part of this book concentrates on rehearsal techniques, with a focus on the physical embodiment and intense joy that can, and should, be generated through working on these plays. I have created and fine-tuned these games, playing them with students and actors at various drama schools, conservatoires and universities in the UK and the USA. Their effectiveness is wholly due to the commitment, talent and hard work of the students I have had the privilege of teaching and directing.

'The wound is open. The wound is peopled' are the last words in a short piece on Shakespeare by Harold Pinter in which he suggests that Shakespeare himself is ultimately unknowable and the mistake too often made is attempting to define him on our own terms. One thing is clear to me, as an actor you must 'keep the wound open' and bring a soulful availability to Shakespeare's words to create the space for the language to resonate. Your emotional reverberation is the bit that no one can teach you; everything else can be learnt.

# A word on punctuation and editions

There is no 'perfect' edition of Shakespeare; in other words there is no irrefutable version from which all punctuation is set out as Shakespeare intended. Quite simply we will never know his intentions; furthermore since the plays come to life through sentient performance, an audience neither hears nor sees the punctuation. Considering that some teachers and directors work from scripts devoid of any punctuation, whilst others don't even believe that a man called Shakespeare wrote these plays, it is worth accepting that you are dealing with an inexact endeavour, within which you must draw your own conclusions as to where the punctuation may originally have been. Every edition of Shakespeare varies depending on the editorial bias and therefore, in terms of punctuation, each edition serves as an informative guide for the actor and director, not as an oracle of truth.

My preferred text is Shakespeare's first folio. It is uncluttered and very beautiful to read. I bought a copy in 2001, together with an excellent dictionary of Shakespeare's words, and these two books have served me through the last fourteen years of teaching, performing and directing. If the first folio is not to your taste, find an edition of Shakespeare's plays that you like and use it with pleasure, making sure it becomes your well-thumbed and intimately known friend. If the punctuation within the speeches in this book doesn't exactly correlate with your version at home or in rehearsal don't panic, it's not a disaster, just follow the exercise and find out what sounds and feels most natural. An audience doesn't come to the theatre to admire your commas, full stops and semi-colons, but rather to follow your thoughts, feelings and emotional resonance. It's worth keeping this in mind as you study the techniques, exercises and games I offer in this book.

**Many of the exercises are accompanied by links to online videos. A list of these links can be found at the back of the book.**

# PART ONE

# RHYTHM, SOUND AND STRUCTURE

These three elements of verse speaking are so inextricably linked that splitting them into separate chapters is somewhat misleading, but also necessary for you to understand each one on its own terms. The rhythm and sound of Shakespeare's words are inseparable and, at the same time, offer different sets of clues as to the changing patterns of a character's thoughts and feelings. Meanwhile the structure of the verse tells you where to breathe and, in doing so, provides you with the means to appear completely spontaneous on stage. Although divided into chapters, consider these elements inseparable from each other – the verse will begin to come to life when the elements in this first part of the book come together.

# 1
# RHYTHM

## Iambic pentameter: The rhythm of your feelings

The first question I ask a new group of students is whether they know what the **iambic pentameter** is and crucially whether they know how to use it as an actor in order to deepen their understanding of their character's inner life. The answers to the first question range from 'It's the dedum dedum dedum thing,' to 'It's the natural way we speak,' (Is it?) to 'I've never heard of it.' There are no conclusive forthcoming answers to the second question. This first chapter is an almost verbatim copy of the way I introduce the iambic and how to use it.

### What exactly is the iambic pentameter?

An iambus is the metrical term for a heartbeat: the natural inner rhythm of the human being and the first sound we hear in the womb. The rhythm has two beats, the first weak and the second strong: **Bu-boom**.

Pentameter means five feet – one foot equals one heartbeat – therefore the rhythm of one line of iambic pentameter, which underpins every line of Shakespeare's blank verse, consists of five heartbeats that have a continual forward momentum.

Bu-_boom_, Bu-_boom_, Bu-_boom_, Bu-_boom_, Bu-_boom_

But the natural speech patterns of Shakespeare's words don't always 'fit' this iambic rhythm and it's within these irregular patterns that you will find initial insights into your character's feelings. To begin to understand how this works, first consider your own heartbeat, a fundamental task because as an actor you must bring your own heart and feelings to your character. The rhythm and rapidity of your heartbeat is constantly changing according to circumstance and emotion; it registers and reflects your feelings often before you have had the time to process your thoughts. For example, if while you were reading this book, a door swung open and a masked attacker entered the room brandishing a weapon and pointing it straight at you, your heart would undoubtedly 'race', 'miss a beat', 'leap to your throat' or indeed 'stop', at least metaphorically. Your understandable fear would register in the disturbed rhythm of your heartbeat, the adrenalin racing around the body forcing the heart into action.

Equally if the same door swung open and the person you had been secretly in love with all your life walked slowly toward you, your heart would undoubtedly register the event. Outwardly you might not move a muscle, but inwardly the movement of your heart would be virtually impossible to ignore. At the very least you might find yourself blushing. Your heart's continual reflection of feelings creates an emotional barometer, registering your own authentic visceral existence. Similarly the changing rhythm of Shakespeare's iambic is an exploration of the personal, intimate experience of life: _it represents the rhythm of your character's feelings_.

Line-by-line, the changing patterns within the rhythm of the verse offer clues as to whether your character's feelings are in their 'natural' state or whether they are heightened and if so by how much. These clues offer psychological insights from which you can start to deepen your understanding of your character's inner life. The key question is this: How do I use the iambic to read these clues? The answer is to become a 'detective of emotion'.

# The emotional detective
# [https://vimeo.com/121688477]

You are going to test out whether the natural rhythm of the words matches the rhythm of the iambic to discover whether your character's feelings are steady or shaken. If the words 'fit' the rhythm, the character can be said to be in the centre of his emotional life. Conversely if the words do not fit and it sounds 'all wrong' to squeeze them into the heartbeat rhythm, then some inner or outer turmoil has shaken the character's feelings. *This will not fundamentally change the way you speak the line; it simply deepens your understanding of it.*

---

### EXERCISE

Take one line of verse at a time. This example from *King Lear* will conclusively establish the technique. As he speaks these words at the end of the play, the old king is holding the dead body of his daughter in his arms; he has reached an apotheosis of pain, anguish and suffering:

Never, never, never, never, never
*King Lear*, 5.3

- To begin, beat out the rhythm of the five heartbeats in any physical way you want, it doesn't matter how you do it – one hand on your chest, both hands on your thighs, drumming your fingers on a table – as long as you ensure you are actually engaging with the rhythm. At the same time whisper the five **Bu-booms** to yourself, so that the rhythm is truly present in your body and voice.

Bu-<u>boom</u>, Bu-<u>boom</u>, Bu-<u>boom</u>, Bu-<u>boom</u>, Bu-<u>boom</u>

This represents a steady emotional rhythm, unchanged by inner or outer turmoil.

- Now speak the line out loud, trying to fit the words to the steady iambic rhythm by emphasizing the syllables that fall on the five strong heartbeats, paying no heed to your natural instinct. Do this quietly, almost whispering so that you can hear and feel the rhythm of the line for yourself. This is the testing part of the exercise. It will sound like this:

Ne<u>ver</u>, ne<u>ver</u>, ne<u>ver</u>, ne<u>ver</u>, ne<u>ver</u>

Ridiculous. It is palpably clear that the line should not be spoken like this. It is not natural.

The key questions in this exercise are: Does it feel and sound completely natural to emphasize these words on the five strong heartbeats? Do the words match the iambic rhythm? Is the character in the centre of his rhythmic emotional life? If not, as is manifestly obvious in this case, the rhythm of the character's feelings are disturbed, changed and shaken.

- Now speak the line again, this time as naturally as possible, paying no heed to the iambic (don't add in any pauses though), so as to confirm for yourself whether any of the naturally emphasized words fall on the strong rhythmic heartbeats. It will very likely have this rhythm running through it:

<u>Ne</u>ver, <u>n</u>ever, <u>n</u>ever, <u>n</u>ever, <u>n</u>ever.

Spoken naturally, the words are in direct opposition with the rhythm of the old king's heartbeat, telling you that his feelings are shaken to their core and that the rhythm with which he speaks is completely 'off the beat', i.e. the naturally emphasized words fall on the weaker beats. These are technically called **inversions** or **trochees**; the rhythm of one heartbeat goes '<u>Bu</u>-boom' as opposed

> to 'Bu-<u>boom</u>'. Think of these inversions as tiny emotional **heart attacks**, or moments of heartbreak. Shakespeare's clue for the actor is in perceiving the rhythm of King Lear's line as five cries of heartbroken pain, relentlessly following one after the other. He *is* broken-hearted and this is directly revealed in the rhythm.

In this example, these tiny heart attacks underpin Lear's heartbroken emotional state, whilst for other characters in other plays, they may signal moments of ecstatic joy when the expression of feeling cannot be contained within the natural iambic rhythm. *A change in rhythm registers a heightened alteration in feeling.* Remember no one in an audience cares what these changes are called; people don't sit in a dark theatre eagerly anticipating inversions and trochees, but they may well remember for many years to come the soulfulness with which you speak the words.

I've chosen this first example to show how watertight the theory is; it would already be obvious that the king's feelings are completely rocked from the overarching plot and Lear's repetition of the single absolute word; in this case the exercise serves to underpin what is already apparent. Not every line of Shakespeare's blank verse is so easy to define as this example of King Lear's. In practice, most lines are made up of a subtle combination of rhythms that give varying clues as to a character's feelings and are, more often than not, part steady, part changeable. These become easier to recognize the more you practise.

Throughout the book we will use Hamlet's first soliloquy:

O that this too too solid flesh would melt
Thaw and resolve itself into a dew
Or that the Everlasting had not fix'd
His canon 'gainst self-slaughter; O God, God!
How weary, stale, flat and unprofitable
Seem to me all the uses of this world.
Fie on't, ah fie, fie! 'Tis an unweeded garden
That grows to seed; things rank and gross in nature

Possess it merely. That it should come to this:
But two months dead: nay, not so much, not two,
So excellent a king; that was, to this
Hyperion to a satyr; so loving to my mother,
That he might not beteem the winds of heaven
Visit her face too roughly. Heaven and earth
Must I remember? Why, she would hang on him,
As if increase of appetite had grown
By what it fed on; and yet within a month?
Let me not think on't: Frailty, thy name is woman.
A little month, or ere those shoes were old
With which she follow'd my poor father's body,
Like Niobe, all tears. Why she, even she,
(O Heaven, a beast that wants discourse of reason
Would have mourn'd longer) married with my uncle,
My father's brother; but no more like my father
Than I to Hercules. Within a month?
Ere yet the salt of most unrighteous tears
Had left the flushing of her galled eyes,
She married. O most wicked speed, to post
With such dexterity to incestuous sheets!
It is not, nor it cannot come to good:
But break, my heart, for I must hold my tongue.
*Hamlet*, 1.2

During the initial work of this exercise, which involves looking at one line at a time, try to make sense of each line by thinking and speaking all the way through to the end, without dropping your vocal and emotional energy. If the line hasn't concluded its meaning, be content for now to leave it unfinished. The sense of many verse lines remains incomplete and it's good practice to get used to how that feels. I use the word 'emphasize' – never the word 'stress'. Think of landing on the empha-sized words in the same way that a tiny bird lands on a twig, lightly arriving and then almost immediately leaving, never clunking down on any one particular word or staying too long.

In the first example, from *King Lear*, we established that a charac-ter's feelings are rocked if the words they speak do not fit naturally with the rhythm of their heartbeat. Conversely if a character's words fit perfectly with the rhythm of the heartbeat, you can determine that they are in the centre of their natural emotional life.

Let's take the last line of Hamlet's speech:

But break, my heart, for I must hold my tongue

- To begin, beat out the rhythm of the five heartbeats in any physical way you want, whispering the five 'Bu-<u>booms</u>' to yourself, so that the rhythm is truly present in your body and voice.

Bu-<u>boom</u> Bu-<u>boom</u> Bu-<u>boom</u> Bu-<u>boom</u> Bu-<u>boom</u>

- Now speak the line out loud, trying to fit the words to the iambic rhythm by emphasizing the syllables that fall on the five strong heartbeats. Do this quietly, almost whispering, so that you can hear and feel the rhythm of the line for yourself. This is the test.

But <u>break,</u> my <u>heart</u>, for <u>I</u> must <u>hold</u> my <u>tongue</u>

In this line the words do indeed fit the rhythm, therefore Hamlet is in a 'natural state' of emotion, and nothing is 'disturbing his heart'. But here you make a huge discovery, natural does not mean neutral; Shakespeare's characters are always emotionally engaged, just as we are in life, whether conscious or indeed asleep. By looking at what he says – making the essential connection between the meaning of the words and the rhythm – we discover that Hamlet's 'natural' emotional state is to embrace his broken heart whilst vowing to stay silent. For lesser characters in other plays, this disturbing emotional state of being may well sway the rhythm of their feelings, but Hamlet owns his broken-hearted pledge of silence as though he were born to it, this *is* his natural emotional state. What a great starting-point for an actor.

# Monosyllables and polysyllables: Prosaic v. poetic

All the words in the above line are **monosyllables** – each word lasts only for one syllable. A little too much is made of these lines in terms of the clues they can give you as an actor; there are far too many monosyllabic lines throughout the plays to warrant one universal technique that will never let you down. They are not a universal signal to 'go slower'. However, it's safe to say that they usually offer a particular prosaic plain quality of thought in direct opposition to lines of fewer words made of more syllables (**polysyllabic**), which are often more poetic or descriptive, such as Hamlet's earlier line:

With such dexterity to incestuous sheets!

Use the difference between the two poetic devices as a clue to show you how much imaginative power your character is using at that moment. I would advise you to take each example on its own merit; the difference between the two does not constitute a universal rule of verse speaking, although it is something worth tuning your ear and eye to as you deepen your understanding of the language. Remember, an audience doesn't come to the theatre merely to praise your monosyllables.

Now let's take the first line of the speech:

O that this too too solid flesh would melt

Hamlet is beginning his contemplation of mortality and suicide, deeply affected by the recent behaviour of his mother.

- Begin once more by physically and vocally engaging with the rhythm:

Bu-<u>boom</u>, Bu-<u>boom</u>, Bu-<u>boom</u>, Bu-<u>boom</u>, Bu-<u>boom</u>

- Now speak the line out loud, trying to fit the words to the iambic rhythm, gently emphasizing the syllables that fall on the five strong heartbeats, whether or not it feels right – this is the test.

O that this too too solid flesh would melt

Ask yourself the same questions as before. Do the words fit naturally to the iambic rhythm?

This one is mixed. Spoken on the beat in this way the first half of the line feels forced and artificial. This immediately lets you know that something is not right with the rhythm of Hamlet's feelings when he begins to speak; you can hear and feel that he is not in the centre of his natural emotional life.

- Therefore speak the line again, this time as unaffectedly as possible, paying no heed to the iambic (don't add in any pauses though), in order to confirm for yourself whether the words fit the rhythm. *Do not feel compelled to keep an even pace through the line, be as changeable and natural as you like.*

It's likely to sound like this:

O that this too too solid flesh would melt

Repeat this as many times as you like. This is not a 'marching army' exercise, in which you must try to stay 'in time'. Speak as naturally as you like, connecting the meaning of the words with the rhythm of the heartbeat, and allowing some words to last a little longer than others. You are looking to see which words fall naturally on the strong heartbeats.

The very first heartbeat is rhythmically reversed, allowing the **O** sound to softly resonate Hamlet's heartbroken feelings. This is another example of the mini heart attacks that Shakespeare so often uses at the beginning of a line, as if to begin to speak entails a moment of heartbreak, allowing the actor to connect with his essential 'open wound'. Towards the end of the line, the natural rhythm of Hamlet's words match the heartbeat rhythm and he regains his emotional centre; this is a very familiar pattern within Shakespeare's verse.

Now look at the first phrase and take time to work through each stage of the exercise on each line; this phrase is four lines long. To understand the coherent sense of a phrase, move from one major punctuation mark all the way through to the next: full stops, question marks and exclamation marks are the major ones to look for. This way you will begin to see larger rhythmic patterns emerge, which give you further clues as to the emotional journey of your character.

My natural rhythms would be as follows:

O that this too too solid flesh would melt
Thaw and resolve itself into a dew
Or that the Everlasting had not fix'd
His canon 'gainst self-slaughter; O God, God!

The first three lines each begin with tiny **heart attacks** and it's not until the fourth line that the pattern changes at the beginning and resumes the natural rhythm. At this point the emotional tension created by the three repetitive 'heart attacks' is released and the natural rhythm of the beginning of the fourth line provides an emotional catharsis. But, by the end of this line, the natural rhythm is once again disturbed, with the repetition of the last word; Hamlet's inner life is rocked by the reiteration of the word **God**. His examination of his relationship with faith, God and religion runs through the play, and can be suggested here, albeit minutely, by how it affects the rhythm of his feelings. This would be my initial interpretation of the changing rhythms; yours will – and should – inevitably be different. This technique is universal; your interpretation will be uniquely yours.

Look at this next phrase; it throws up some fresh challenges.

How weary, stale, flat and unprofitable
Seem to me all the uses of this world.

The natural delivery of this phrase can be debated. It's within this debate that the technique of the detective work merges with interpretation, which is perhaps the most pleasurable and sophisticated part of unpicking Shakespeare's rhythms. This work is not an exact science; it is an artistic endeavour.

First do the detective work.

- Beat out the rhythm of the heartbeats:

Bu-<u>boom</u>, Bu-<u>boom</u>, Bu-<u>boom</u>, Bu-<u>boom</u>, Bu-<u>boom</u>

- Now speak the words, trying as hard as you can to fit them to the perfect iambic rhythm:

How <u>wea</u>ry, <u>stale</u>, flat <u>and</u> un<u>pro</u>fi<u>ta</u>ble
Seem <u>to</u> me <u>all</u> the <u>u</u>ses <u>of</u> this <u>world</u>.

Do the words fit naturally to the rhythm? Does it feel completely natural to emphasize the words that fall on the five strong heartbeats?

Spoken on the beat in this way, the lines sound forced and not a little stuffy. Not all the words fit naturally on the rhythm, so you can immediately establish that this phrase causes Hamlet grief, creating a rhythmic mirror to his sentiment.

- Now speak the line again, this time as naturally as possible (don't add any pauses within the line) paying no heed to the iambic. Confirm for yourself whether any of the words land on the strong heartbeats. Begin to connect the meaning of the words to the rhythm of the heartbeat.

Your natural reading may go like this:

How <u>wea</u>ry, <u>stale</u>, <u>flat</u> and un<u>pro</u>fitable
<u>Seem</u> to <u>me</u> <u>all</u> the <u>u</u>ses of this <u>world</u>.

The first line sounds natural enough; the words are falling on some strong heartbeats but not on others, signalling a rocked inner life and a therefore a deep emotional engagement to this sentiment. However, I have only highlighted four strong beats and, spoken with this rhythm, there is a danger that the phrase can sound recited, as if Hamlet has already had this thought process and is recounting it. This may well send the audience to sleep.

By adding a fifth (and arguably necessary) beat, this next version emphasizes the word **and**, which falls on a strong heartbeat and forces Hamlet into thinking on his feet.

How <u>weary</u>, <u>stale</u>, <u>flat</u> <u>and</u> unpr<u>ofi</u>table
<u>Seem</u> to <u>me</u> <u>all</u> the <u>us</u>es of this <u>world.</u>

Giving life to the word **and** has the effect of making Hamlet appear
to be thinking in the moment, perfectly embodying Shakespeare's
dynamic movement of thought from mind to mouth. Emphasizing
the little, connecting words will often make the difference between
sounding as if you are reciting something you have learnt and sounding
as if you freshly imagined it at the very moment you spoke it. The word
**all** in the second line has the same energizing effect.

Try two versions. First speak the phrase without emphasizing the
words **and** and **all**. Secondly speak the phrase with an emphasis on
both these words, allowing the emphasis to reinforce the idea that you
are having these thoughts for the very first time. Don't overemphasize;
this rhythmic work is never about raising the volume of your voice, it's
about deepening your experience of thought to the word. Sometimes
just thinking about the word will make the difference. It's useful to test
the two different versions out for yourself so you can personally feel the
difference.

The power of the tiny word **all** is revealed in the second line.
Emphasizing this word can have a transformative effect, lifting you
from the ordinary to the absolute and allowing you to experience a
heightened state of emotion. Look out for this word; in one short
syllable it can explosively bring you and your character to life. (We will
explore the power of the little words further in Chapter 6.)

**The emotional detective** gives you a solid foundation from which
to begin to build an understanding of the inner life of your character;
your thorough knowledge of the rhythm of every line potentially offers
a secret relationship with the words you speak. With practise and
experience, you will almost immediately recognize how Shakespeare
reveals the rhythm of your character's feelings without having to stop
and do this exercise on every line. If you are new to this work, give
yourself the time to develop the skill.

*Do not feel compelled to keep an even pace through each line. It
is essential to own the language for yourself. Be as changeable and
natural as you like, you are in charge of the rhythm – it is not in charge
of you.*

# Masculine or feminine: Purpose v. doubt

Look again at the rhythm of this line:

How weary, stale, flat and unprofitable

Unlike the other lines we have looked at so far, it does not have a strong beat at its end. Traditionally lines with 'weak endings', such as these, are known as **feminine**, whereas lines that end with strong one-syllable words are known as **masculine**. This is not exclusive to Shakespeare, but rather is an acknowledged poetic practice. The odd-numbered lines do indeed have weak-sounding endings, but there is nothing for the actor to gain emotionally or intellectually by thinking of this weakness as feminine.

Shakespeare created some of the strongest female characters in dramatic literature, as well as some of the weakest males, therefore to equate weakness with femininity and vice versa within the structure of his blank verse does not serve any purpose. It's more useful to view the strong ending of a line as having definition and purpose, whilst weak endings offer the opportunity to explore a moment of doubt.

# How do I practise the iambic rhythm?

Musicians practise scales every day and dancers take a daily class. This exercise gives you the opportunity to practise the iambic rhythm of the verse, so it can begin to become second nature. It is a technical exercise equivalent to the plié of the dancer and the scales of the pianist. Fortunately for the actor you do not need an instrument or a dance studio, you can do it alone under your breath, waiting at a bus stop or walking through a park. It is quite simply – practice.

## EXERCISE

### The glockenspiel

Take one line of verse where the words fit naturally on the iambic rhythm. The exercise is *not* of benefit with lines of verse that do not fit. Let's go back to the last line of Hamlet's speech:

But <u>break,</u> my <u>heart,</u> for <u>I</u> must <u>hold</u> my <u>tongue.</u>

Repeat the line five times. Each time emphasize *one* of the strong heartbeats, progressing from the first through to the last.

But **break**, my heart, for I must hold my tongue.
But break, my **heart**, for I must hold my tongue.
But break, my heart, for **I** must hold my tongue.
But break, my heart, for I must **hold** my tongue.
But break, my heart, for I must hold my **tongue**.

Try two different ways of using your breath with the **glockenspiel** exercise:

1. Breathe at the end of every line.
2. Take one deep breath and try to speak all five lines.

We will make an in-depth investigation of where to breathe in Chapter 4.

This exercise is a means of practising your technique and ensuring the iambic rhythm becomes as organic as possible. I am not suggesting that you would prepare for a performance by planning to 'emphasize number three and number four'. In fact the opposite is true, the exercise will allow you to have the rhythm at your fingertips in performance, knowing that whichever word or words you emphasize will make emotional and intellectual sense. It may be that in rehearsal you (and the director) decide upon a very particular delivery, but until then keep your options open. As well as being an excellent exercise for getting the iambic rhythm into your sense memory, this is a great line-learning technique. I guarantee that you will know the line after two or three goes.

The following lines from Hamlet's speech are also perfect for this exercise.

But two months dead: nay, not so much, not two

As if increase of appetite had grown

A little month, or ere those shoes were old

Ere yet the salt of most unrighteous tears
Had left the flushing of her galled eyes,

It is not, nor it cannot come to good:
But break, my heart, for I must hold my tongue

It's useful to see where these natural lines of iambic fall within the speech as a whole. They often land between two lines that are 'off the beat', creating a tidal effect, pushing and pulling the rhythm of Hamlet's feelings to match the sense and content of the speech.

## EXERCISE

### Brain on/brain off

First do the **glockenspiel** exercise with your brain fully engaged: consciously think about the particular word you are emphasizing and let it affect the way you feel when you say the line. You should find that this same line has five completely different readings, depending on the word you commit to. It should feel different each time. Think of this as exploding and discovering the emotional and intellectual energy of a line.

Secondly, do the exercise with your 'brain turned off'. Repeat the words, but without making an effort to commit to their sense and feeling.

Alternate between the two, consciously turning your brain 'off' and 'on' at will and noticing the difference between the two versions. The first one will encourage you to discover the level of commitment necessary to bring one line to life, demonstrating how much mental and emotional energy you need in order to begin to act. The second version is there to remind you how easy it is to be lazy, so that you can feel the difference for yourself. Don't wait to be told; be your own taskmaster.

It's essential to genuinely engage your brain when you are acting and never 'coast' through any text. Shakespeare's language sometimes has a 'deadening' effect on actors, as if the rhythm sends them to sleep. Endeavour to remain alive to what you are saying, allowing yourself to be changed by the experience of speaking the words, thinking the thoughts and feeling the emotions. This exercise provides an excellent way of experiencing the difference for yourself to ensure that you remain switched on. It is a potent acting experience and can be applied to every technique throughout the book.

# The changing rhythm throughout Shakespeare's plays

If you were presented with a speech from a Shakespeare play, would you know if it was written in the early, middle or late years of his career? Shakespeare developed as a playwright over the course of nearly 24 years, so much so that the experience of acting in *The Taming of the*

*Shrew* (an early play) is almost entirely different from that of being in *A Winter's Tale* (a late play). Nowhere is this so obvious as in the differences in the rhythm of the verse. Broadly speaking, characters in the early plays speak with relatively simple rhythms, which stay close to the natural iambic throughout. These are far removed from the sophistication of the middle and late plays, in which complex changing patterns of rhythm reveal emotional states and psychological insights *in extremis*.

It follows that if you are going to be in his plays, you must know when Shakespeare wrote them; the exact date is not essential, but a knowledge of how the plays group together will be an extremely useful tool. For this reason I am placing this chronology here and I strongly recommend you make acquaintance with it, making it an active part of your understanding of Shakespeare.

| | |
|---|---|
| *The Two Gentlemen of Verona* | 1589–91 |
| *The Taming of the Shrew* | 1590–1 |
| *King Edward II* with other authors | 1590–4 |
| *Henry VI Part II* | 1590–1 |
| *Henry VI Part III* | 1591 |
| *Henry VI Part I* | 1592 |
| *Titus Andronicus* | 1592 |
| *Richard III* | 1594 |
| *The Comedy of Errors* | 1594 |
| *Love's Labour's Lost* | 1594–5 |
| *Richard II* | 1595 |
| *Romeo and Juliet* | 1595 |
| *A Midsummer Night's Dream* | 1595 |
| *King John* | 1596 |
| *The Merchant of Venice* | 1596–7 |
| *Henry IV Part I* | 1596–7 |
| *The Merry Wives of Windsor* | 1597–8 |
| *Henry IV Part II* | 1597–8 |
| *Much Ado About Nothing* | 1598–9 |
| *Henry V* | 1598–9 |
| *Julius Caesar* | 1599 |
| *As You Like It* | 1599–1600 |
| *Hamlet* | 1600–1 |

| | |
|---|---|
| *Twelfth Night* | 1601 |
| *Troilus and Cressida* | 1602 |
| *Measure for Measure* | 1603–4 |
| *Othello* | 1603–4 |
| *King Lear* | 1605–6 |
| *Timon of Athens* | 1606 |
| *Macbeth* | 1606 |
| *Antony and Cleopatra* | 1606 |
| *All's Well That Ends Well* | 1606–7 |
| *Pericles* | 1607 |
| *Coriolanus* | 1608 |
| *The Winter's Tale* | 1609–10 |
| *Cymbeline* | 1610–11 |
| *The Tempest* | 1610–11 |
| *Henry VIII* with John Fletcher | 1613 |
| *The Two Noble Kinsmen* with John Fletcher | 1613 |

This order of plays is concluded by Stanley Wells and Gary Taylor in their *Complete Oxford Shakespeare* (Oxford: Clarendon Press, 2005), with the addition of *Edward II*. The dates in many cases are significantly earlier than the date of the first known publication or performance.

The iambic pentameter signals the rhythm of your character's feelings, but it only starts to feel spontaneous and natural when practised in conjunction with the sound and structure of the words that make up the fabric of the language. As you read on, use what you have learnt about the rhythm to inform your acting and come back to these basic exercises whenever you feel the need to test out your instinct about a line.

# 2
# SOUND

Shakespeare is often introduced to acting students in a voice class, where the emphasis may be placed on *how* to make a sound rather than *why*. It's undeniable that voices can be improved and developed; however this book already assumes a level of vocal ability and concentrates instead on how to discover the profound acting clues that exist in the sound patterns of Shakespeare's language.

Your unique voice is one of your most powerful means of expressing yourself; please do not think you have to modify your accent in order to achieve some idea of 'good Shakespeare speaking'. This book encourages you to explore your own natural sounds, so you can begin to experience how to generate the language for yourself, wherever your accent may originally spring from.

## Alliteration

Once you have begun to interpret the clues in the rhythm of the language, as set out in the previous chapter, it is essential to do the same with the sound; an understanding of Shakespeare's use of

**alliteration** is a perfect place to start. As babies, we are introduced to language alliteratively. The adults around us say, 'boo boo boo', 'coo coo coo', 'moo moo moo', alerting our ears to communicative sound patterns, in order for us to begin to understand the world. In Shakespeare's plays, alliteration works in the same way: the repetitions and patterns of sounds alert the audience to the language being spoken. There are two major ways you can use the alliteration to discover your character's thoughts and emotions. The first exercise explores how alliterative phrases reveal the pace and temperature of your thoughts, whilst the second shows how they provide a thread of emotional and intellectual sense through a phrase.

---

## EXERCISE

### The speed of thought
### [https://vimeo.com/121688479]

Alliteration can be understood as speed of thought, or more usefully the temperature of your thought – whether it is hot or cold. The more densely alliterative the phrase, the quicker it is borne out of you, as if your mind is on fire. Conversely, if the alliteration is more evenly spaced, or indeed absent, you can afford to speak more slowly, as if the thoughts are chipped from ice and taking longer to be formed. As with all rules, this one can of course be bent and broken, but I would strongly recommend you use it when you first work on a speech. It is essential to discover explosive changes of pace within the language and, by following the alliteration, you'll find that Shakespeare points them out to you in abundance.

Staying with Hamlet's first soliloquy, let's take this phrase:

**Fie** on't, ah **fie, fie!** 'Tis an unweeded garden
That **grows** to seed; things rank and **gross** in nature
Possess it merely.
*Hamlet*, 1.2

---

Note the mini **heart attack** at the beginning of the first line. Look at the alliteration, searching for where it is densely packed and where it is spaced apart. You can underline it in your script if that helps; I usually draw circles around alliterative patterns.

The alliteration is densely packed to start with and explodes at the beginning of the phrase:

**Fie** on't, ah **fie**, **fie!**

This hot-headed explosiveness is immediately followed by a phrase that contains only one alliterative connection, between **grows** and **gross**. The absence of other alliteration has the effect of Hamlet slowly calming himself, creating the space and time to carve out the mind's eye image of the fetid garden.

'Tis an unweeded garden
That **grows** to seed; things rank and **gross** in nature
Possess it merely.

Speak the lines out loud twice, trying to feel the difference for yourself between the two versions. First pay no heed to the alliteration and keep an even, steady pace all the way through. Secondly speak the lines again, this time following the speed of thought as set out by the alliteration, attacking the beginning with a hot speed, where the alliteration is densely packed, and consciously slowing down when it is evenly spaced.

The alliterative patterns increase with the next phrase:

Tha**t** it should come to **th**is:
But **two months** dead: **nay**, **not** so **much**, **not two**,

The alliteration intensifies and culminates with a second fiery explosion wherein Hamlet upbraids himself for getting the facts wrong with **nay**, **not** and **not**.

> Now put the phrase together and speak it out loud, following the pace of the alliteration; speeding up when it is densely packed and allowing the words to be borne out of you slowly when it is evenly spaced or absent. Connect the meaning of the words with the patterns of alliteration as you speak. It is as if the slow-borne images of Hamlet's thoughts are sandwiched between his fast emotional outbursts, each existing because of the other.

These changes in pace provide you with starting-points for your own psychological interpretation and understanding of Hamlet's thoughts and emotions within this short phrase. The lightning speed with which he changes from fire to ice is universal to Shakespeare's language: it is as if a character has two voices in conversation with one another in his or her mind. Shakespeare often uses this device, especially in the soliloquies, which you can think of as 'the conversation of my thoughts', as described by Helena in *All's Well that Ends Well* (1.3).

Sometimes, not all the alliterative words fall naturally on the emphasized beats – technically this is known as **consonance**. If *all* the similar-sounding words that begin with the same letter fall on the naturally strong beats, this is alliterative. Use this **speed of thought** technique whether the words are on the beat or off; an audience does not come to the theatre to praise your knowledge of alliteration, but they may well be mesmerized by your ability to embrace the fire and ice of Hamlet's changeability. Remember to employ discretion; these are subtle adjustments, neither the slow nor the fast should be exaggerated or appear forced. It is better to think of fire and ice rather than fast versus slow. You are adjusting Hamlet's speed of *thought* not his speed of *speech*. We speak because we think!

If you are working in groups or with a partner you can split the speech up between you, one half speaking the 'fire' and the other half speaking the 'ice'.

# Finding the thread of sense

Shakespeare creates alliterative patterns that lead you to one final word as a pinnacle of emotion and thought. This exercise shows how you can use these patterns to discover your character's thread of sense and alert the audience's ears to what is important.

---

## EXERCISE

### Making a scaffolding

A **scaffolding** is a short pattern of words that you remove from a speech in order to practise them out loud and get them into your sense memory. They allow you to experience how the language continually moves forward, creating emotional and intellectual peaks. After you have practised a scaffolding by itself, you return to the full speech, incorporating the pattern of words to highlight the thread of sense and thereby increasing the emotional and intellectual intensity.
  Here's a longer phrase from Hamlet's speech.

- Follow the words that begin with **M**:

  (O Heaven, a beast that wants discourse of reason
  Would have **mourn'd** longer) **married** with **my** uncle
  **My** father's brother; but no **more** like **my** father
  Than I to Hercules. Within a **month?**

- Make a scaffolding from the seven words:

  mourned, married, my, my, more, my, month

At first sight the list appears to be seven abstract words, but on closer inspection, you will find that Gertrude's actions and Hamlet's feelings are buried deep within the pattern.

---

- Speak and repeat the seven words with an increased emotional intensity, driving toward the last one; each word causes Hamlet increasing anguish. If you speak them as a flat list with no climactic energy, they will lack emotional and intellectual energy and when you return the words to the full phrase the exercise will not have worked.

  Bring commitment to the scaffolding exercise, otherwise it will be of no benefit, but let your acting be discreet; he is feeling pain, not showing it. At this point, you can also speak the words of the scaffolding using the **brain on/brain off** exercise as described in Chapter 1.

- Repeat the scaffolding on its own a few last times, concentrating on the drive towards the last word.
- Now speak the whole phrase, incorporating the words of the scaffolding, to explore the sense of your freshly discovered emotional thread.

You can create these scaffoldings from any phrase in Shakespeare in order to explore the thread of sense over a few lines. When choosing the words, ensure that they begin with the same letter – some will fall on the beat and some will fall off the beat – the last one should be at the end of a phrase and provide a climactic moment. Speak and repeat the scaffolding, so that the drive towards the last word is locked in your sense memory. Then replace the words and speak the lines all the way through, allowing the words of the scaffolding to provide the drive through to the end of the phrase.

# Rhyme

Beware of self-consciously over-emphasizing the rhymes in Shakespeare – specifically at the ends of lines and in the rhyming couplets of the earlier plays. Use these as a way of alerting the audience to meaning and character as much as you can, rather than producing empty rhyming patterns. For example, you can guard against appearing merely descriptive with these lines of Oberon's by truly engaging with what he sees in his mind's eye, allowing the rhyme to take care of itself. This is a theme that will come up repeatedly throughout the book.

OBERON
I know a bank where the wild thyme blows,
　　　Where oxlips and the nodding violet grows,

Quite o'ercanopied with luscious woodbine

With sweet musk roses and with eglantine.
*A Midsummer Night's Dream*, 2.1

An investigation of repetitive vowels sounds inside the words – technically known as **assonance** – can yield a richer source of psychological starting-points. In this next example there is an internal rhyming pattern on the sound of **O**, which deepens the quality of grief to match the meaning of the character's words.

GERTRUDE
One **woe** doth tread upon another's heel

**So** fast they foll**ow**. Your sister's drowned, Laertes.
LAERTES
Drowned? **O**, where?
GERTRUDE
There is a willow **grows** aslant a brook
That **shows** its hoar leaves in the glassy stream.
Hamlet, 4.7

You can create a scaffolding here that could be spoken by one actor or shared by both:

woe – so – ow – O – grows – shows

The climax of this scaffolding is in fact on the 'O'. Gertrude's next two words are almost like echoes to their shared pain.

# Isolating the vowels

There is a well-used maxim that vowels hold the emotion of a word, while the consonants contain the sense. I will investigate this further in the next chapter; meanwhile an excellent exploration of vowel sounds can be achieved through this exercise.

## EXERCISE

Take one line at a time. Speak the line out loud, checking the rhythm, sound and consonants. Let's look at this line:

LEAR
Howl, howl, howl, howl! O, you are men of stones.

*King Lear*, 5.3

Slowly and quietly repeat the line, omitting the consonants and making only the sounds of vowels. Initially the exercise should be almost internal. *It is not an exercise in voice production; it is an investigation into the emotional experience of making these sounds.* It will sound something like this:

ow ... ow ... ow ... ow ... O ... OOO ... ah ... e ... O ... oh

The exercise gives you the chance to know the pattern that the sounds make. In this line, the central journey of 'ow ... O ... OOO' seems to offer an aural depiction of grief. It is also useful to see that there is an internal rhyme between the word O and the sound of O inside the word 'stone' at the end. Before you can hope to project these details to an audience or even other actors, you must *know and feel* them for yourself. This exercise gives you the chance to practise. Repeat this as often as you need to.

Now use the **brain on/brain off** technique. First, consciously think about the words as you are making the sounds, committing as deeply as you can to the thought and connecting the thought to the emotion. Do your best acting here, not indulgent but deeply committed; the only thing that is missing is the consonants.

Secondly, turn your brain off and simply repeat the sounds. Alternate between the two, so that you understand and experience for yourself how hard you have to work to achieve the 'brain on' version, connecting thought and emotion.

Finally, go back to the line, adding the consonants back in. You should aim to be able to articulate a line without consonants at a moment's notice. Develop this skill, so that you can speak an entire speech, or indeed your whole part, with or without consonants with consummate ease.

Vowel sounds are indeed the heart and soul of expressive feeling, but must always be produced as a result of thought and emotion. Your connection to your vowels is a connection to the inside of yourself. Nothing less.

## The howl sound

When you come across this sound, stop and investigate. It is at the centre of Shakespeare's verse and relates directly to human pain and suffering *in extremis*. It should not be ignored. Here are a few more examples:

GERTRUDE
Your sister's **drowned**, Laertes.
LAERTES
**Drowned**? O, where?

Alas, then is she **drowned**.
GERTRUDE
**Drowned, drown'd.**
*Hamlet*, 4.7

CLAUDIUS
**Bow** stubborn knees and heart with strings of steel

Be soft as sinews of the new-born babe
*Hamlet*, 3.3

ROSALIND
Pray you no more of this, 'tis like the **howl**ing of Irish wolves against
the moon.
*As You Like It*, 5.2

Is this Shakespeare's reminder to us all to check against indulgence?

You can use vocal exercises to practise this howl sound, but no technique can tell you how to actually access it emotionally. It may be one of the great tests of the Shakespearean actor: to remain emotionally open enough to *feel the wound* and just about sane enough to relate it to others.

An understanding of how the outward form of rhythm and sound come together is essential in order to begin to take possession of the language for yourself. At best, the exercises in these first two chapters begin to demonstrate how the life force of a human being can be expressed through Shakespeare's language and how it is completely necessary to be present when speaking the words. Return to these chapters as often as you need; these early exercises will become easier as your understanding of the language increases. Meanwhile continue with the rest of Part One to bring the three fundamental elements of verse speaking together.

# 3
# THE EMOTIONAL ALPHABET

EXERCISE

- Your own emotional alphabet

Taking ownership of Shakespeare's language is a fundamental part of the actor's skill; the words are all you have to begin to express the full landscape of human emotion as prescribed by Shakespeare. Moreover you must express them with a clarity that will convince a potential thousand-seater audience of your authenticity. It all starts with your relationship to the words. In 2001, when I was performing at the RSC, I created an alphabet of emotions – in a diary I wrote down letters of the alphabet, giving each an idiosyncratic title that described a particular feeling, followed by examples of phrases and lines from plays that I was working on. I've been using it ever since.

In Chapter 2 I introduced the well-used maxim that vowels contain the feeling of a word while the consonants contain the sense. Although the five vowels and all their beautiful mixes are indeed a rich source of soulfulness for the actor, I don't believe this to be at the expense of consonants. Vowels are indeed the articulation of emotions within the human voice; emotions that are made specific by the consonants. Nowhere is this better proven than in swearwords, most notably the **F** and **C** word. You can swap the vowel sounds for both those one-syllable words and it will make no difference – it will still feel damn good to swear. In the context of Shakespeare's language, this maxim doesn't take into account the emotive power of **alliteration**, which relies mainly on consonants. Ignore Shakespeare's emotive consonants at your peril.

My alphabet of emotions concentrates on the consonants and has led me to investigate their effects on the speaking actor, the listening actor and – essentially – the audience. This list has shown me the regular patterns of consonants Shakespeare uses throughout the plays; he has favourite consonants to swear with and those with which to express love, warmth and grief. He has some favourite **digraphs** too (a fancy word for two consonants elided together). All these are instantly recognizable if you know where to look.

Below is an edited version of my alphabet of emotions to give you an idea of how it works. I use it throughout the book, so the names are worth memorizing. The examples I've given are all personal to me; some are alliterative, whilst others show how the single use of the sound brings a phrase to life. I have experienced first-hand connections with all of them through acting, teaching and directing the plays.

The phrases from *Pyramus and Thisbe* in *A Midsummer Night's Dream* serve as Shakespeare's own satire on his art form and a reminder never to take yourself too seriously.

# The emotional alphabet

As you read my alphabet, take the time to quietly repeat the pure sounds to yourself, attempting to deeply connect to the primary emotion the sound creates within you.

## B: The bastard sound

EDMUND
Why bastard? Wherefore base?
… Why brand they us
with base, with baseness, bastardy, base, base
    *King Lear*, 1.2

QUINCE (as PROLOGUE)
Whereat, with blade, with bloody, blameful, blade,
He bravely broach'd his boiling bloody breast.
*A Midsummer Night's Dream*, 5.1

## D: The sound of death

GHOST
I am thy father's spirit,
Doomed for a certain term to walk the night

*Hamlet,* 1.5

BOTTOM
Now, die, die, die, die, die.
*A Midsummer Night's* Dream, 5.1

MACBETH
I have done the deed.

*Macbeth,* 2.2

## F: The greatest sound to swear with

Shakespeare uses his own f\*\*k sound to incredible effect. It is naturally quiet and thereby phenomenally powerful as a means to swear. More than often he places the **F** words on mighty strong heartbeats, allowing the actor to let rip, but because it is a truly quiet sound it prevents you from shouting. This first example is as if Hamlet is swearing under his breath.

HAMLET
Fie on't, ah fie, fie!
*Hamlet*, 1.2

CALIBAN
All the infections that the sun sucks up
From bogs, fens, flats, on Prosper fall
*The Tempest*, 2.2.

LEAR
Blasts and fogs upon thee!
*King Lear*, 1.4

GHOST
And for the day confined to fast in fires
*Hamlet, 1.5*

## *H: The sound of breath and whispers*

EDGAR
And by the happy hollow of a tree
　　　Escaped the hunt.

*King Lear, 2.3*

GHOST
O, horrible, O, horrible, most horrible!
*Hamlet, 1.5*

## *K (and hard C): The sound of killing*

LEAR
And when I have stol'n upon these sons-in-law,
　　　then, kill, kill, kill, kill, kill, kill!
　　　　　　*King Lear, 4.6*

## *L: The sound of love*

I hear a sing-song tune when I repeat the sound of **L**, something like church bells – 'la la la laah'. For me this is most potent when the character speaking is in turmoil. The sound is sweet, but the wound is open.

ORLANDO
Live a little, comfort a little, cheer thyself a little.
　　　*As You Like It, 2.6*

PROSPERO
We are such stuff
As dreams are made on, and our little life
is rounded with a sleep.
*The Tempest, 4.1*

## M: The mother sound

The warmest sound you can make in the English language; the almost universal sound for the naming of mothers, the **M** sound creates a humming in the mouth and voice that no other sound does. Try to say any word that begins with M without humming – it is impossible, you will always sound at your warmest. It's also the sound of possession; 'me' 'myself' and 'mine' all create an unconscious humming on the lips. Conversely it is the sound for two prominent words and themes throughout the plays: murder and madness.

CALIBAN
This island's mine, by Sycorax my mother,
Which thou tak'st from me.
*The Tempest*, 1.2

## N: The sound of 'no'

This is the almost universal sound of negativity.

HAMLET
nay, not so much, not two
*Hamlet*, 1.2

LEAR
never, never, never, never, never.

*King Lear*, 5.3

## St: The sound of the stars

Shakespeare often uses a double **st** ... **st** effect, which creates the twinkling sensation of stars.

HELENA

By the luckiest stars in heaven
*All's Well That Ends Well*, 1.3

## S: The almost silent sound

DUKE FREDERICK
Not seen him since? Sir, sir, that cannot be.
*As You Like It*, 3.1

## Sh: The second greatest sound to swear with

The close second to the **F** sound.

HAMLET
Why she, even she
*Hamlet*, 1.2

HAMLET
She married.
*Hamlet*, 1.2

## Sp: The sound of the spirit

GHOST
I am thy father's spirit.
*Hamlet,* 1.5

## W: The sound of woe

HAMLET
Woo't weep? Woo't fight? Woo't fast? Woo't tear thyself?
Woo't drink up easel, eat a crododile?
I'll do't.
*Hamlet*, 5.1

## EXERCISE

### Your own emotional alphabet
### [https://vimeo.com/121688482]

I strongly recommend you create your own alphabet of emotions. It is not an academic document, far from it, but rather your personal response to Shakespeare, which will develop as you begin to experience how the plays seem to talk to each other in pattern, sound, theme, rhythm and character. Not all the consonants of the alphabet need to be there, this isn't a school exercise, put them in if and when they become pertinent to you.

Once these deeper connections with Shakespeare's sounds start to resonate in your sense memory, the emotional life of the language will begin to become visible when you see the words on the page. Shakespeare's language is much more than a beautiful sounding collection of words, it is a dance of human emotions, the alchemy of which exists in their collisions. Your task is to catch these collisions and bring them to life, for example, the sound of **breath** colliding with the **mother** sound:

FERDINAND
Here's my hand.
MIRANDA
And mine, with my heart in't.
*The Tempest*, 3.1

And again:

CONSTANCE
I am not mad, this hair I tear is mine
*King John*, 3.4

The **mother** sound colliding with the greatest sound to **swear** with:

GHOST
        Revenge his foul and most unnatural murder.
HAMLET
            Murder?
GHOST

Murder most foul, as in the best it is.

But this most foul, strange and unnatural.
*Hamlet*, 1.5

The sound of **love** colliding with the **mother** sound:

HAMLET
I have of late, but wherefore I know not, lost all my mirth.

*Hamlet*, 2.2

And see these collisions for yourself:

LEAR
Thou art a soul in bliss, but I am bound
Upon a wheel of fire, that mine own tears
Do scald like molten lead.

*King Lear*, 4.7

# 4

# STRUCTURE: WHEN DO I BREATHE?

EXERCISES

- The thinking breath
- The changing lines
- Doubling
- Last words

*Shakespeare's intellectual action is wholly unlike that of Ben Jonson or Beaumont or Fletcher. The latter see the totality of a sentence or a passage, and then project it entire. Shakespeare goes on creating, and evolving B out of A, and C out of B, and so on, just as a serpent moves, which makes a fulcrum of its own body, and seems for ever twisting and untwisting its own strength.*

S. T. Coleridge, *Table Talk* (1834)

*Twisting and untwisting its own strength*! The greatest description of the experience of speaking blank verse I have ever come across. It is, in other words, unstoppable.

It would seem that nothing divides actors, students, teachers, directors and sometimes even audience members more than the question of when the Shakespearean actor should take a breath. The only thing everyone agrees upon is that the actor must breathe at some point to avoid collapsing.

Shakespeare's blank verse can be understood as a continuous unfolding of thought – only death can stop the characters needing to think and speak, and even then some will return as ghosts with more to say. In essence the verse never stops and the characters never cease to think, feel and exist; they always have more to say. Thinking and breathing exist alongside each other, therefore the answer to 'When do I breathe?' lies in the exploration of how we think and Shakespeare has laid that out for us in within the *structure* of the verse.

# The thinking breath [https://vimeo.com/121688483]

At the end of every verse line is a potential **thinking breath**, a moment when the character actively thinks and breathes at the same time. The physical experience of the thinking breath is the experience of the mind actively moving forward, it is not a stopping, it is barely a pause.

## EXERCISE

As the first step, you are going to think and breathe at the end of every line of verse. *Don't panic, you would never do this in performance – this is an initial exercise.* I've specifically chosen a speech from *The Tempest*, one of Shakespeare's last plays, as the verse structure is complicated and requires real technique to keep sense and feeling alive.

To begin, take the first complete phrase of the speech; remember a complete phrase is one that goes from one major punctuation mark to the next. Here's the speech:

CALIBAN
All the infections that the sun sucks up
From bogs, fens, flats, on Prosper fall and make him

By inchmeal a disease! His spirits hear me
And yet I needs must curse. But they'll nor pinch,
Fright me with urchin-shows, pitch me i' th' mire,
Nor lead me like a firebrand in the dark
Out of my way, unless he bid 'em. But
For every trifle are they set upon me,
Sometime like apes that mow and chatter at me,
And after bite me, then like hedgehogs which
Lie tumbling in my barefoot way and mount
Their pricks at my footfall. Sometime am I
All wound with adders who with cloven tongues
Do hiss me into madness. Lo, now, lo!
Here comes a spirit of his, and to torment me
For bringing wood in slowly. I'll fall flat.
Perchance he will not mind me.
*The Tempest*, 2.2

Take the first complete phrase:

All the infections that the sun sucks up
From bogs, fens, flats, on Prosper fall and make him
By inchmeal a disease!

At the end of each line think and breathe. Breathe *because* you are thinking. It takes no longer than a click of your fingers, a split-second; in fact you can click your fingers at the same time if it helps. Very specifically, this thinking can be paraphrased as, 'What words do I say next to best express my thoughts and feelings?' or 'How do I say what I want to say next?' This precisely mirrors how we think and speak in normal life; we do not have speeches written for us and we very often pause in the middle of what we are saying in order to collect our thoughts; at those moments we take an involuntary breath. It is recognizably human. Shakespeare has given you an opportunity to do just this. And each one is a potential acting opportunity.

Now speak the phrase again without the thinking breaths.
Alternate between the two – taking thinking breaths and not taking
breaths – for as long as you need, so that you begin to experience
the difference for yourself. Without the thinking breaths, the line
will feel recited, as if Caliban already knows what he is going to
say. The phrase will not live. With the thinking breaths, you have
the opportunity to exist as a sentient being, actively engaged in *the
invention of language.*

Following the verse structure by thinking and breathing at the end of
the lines will have the effect of making you seem completely natural,
as if you are making up the words as you go along. This is the ultimate
example of using technique to appear spontaneous. It is often said that
Shakespeare's iambic rhythm mirrors our natural patterns of speech; in
my experience it is actually the structure of the verse and the thinking
breath that best represent the way we communicate.

To reassure you: you wouldn't take a thinking breath after every line
in performance; this is an exercise to allow you to initially explore the
potential acting opportunities Shakespeare has given you.

Be brave. During this initial exercise use the thinking breath (which
you must keep very short) to experience a 'white brain' moment; a
split second of not knowing at all what your next words will be. You
know what you want to say, but haven't found the words. In this way,
the thinking breath serves as a moment of mental re-energizing and
the next line has a renewed vigour. This really helps with exploring
the rhythm of the heartbeat; in this first phrase, Caliban naturally
emphasizes the first strong heartbeats of the second and third lines,
and landing on the words *bog* and *inch* becomes a mini-cathartic
experience.

## Changing or bridging lines

Take a look at the third line of Caliban's speech above:

By inchmeal a disease! His spirits hear me

The sense of this phrase finishes half-way through the verse line. And the second half of the verse line is the beginning of another thought, which itself finishes half-way through the following verse line! This is precisely why I chose this speech. As I said in Chapter 1, the rhythm and verse structure of Shakespeare's early plays is simple; most characters finish most of their thoughts at the end of verse lines and begin their thoughts at the beginning of the next. It's useful to think of this as being **on the verse**. By the time Shakespeare wrote *The Tempest*, he had created and mastered the technique of characters speaking **through the verse**.

The technical term for a punctuation mark in the middle of a line that signals a change of thought is a **caesura**. The vast majority of the audience will not know that and none of the audience has come to the theatre to specifically admire your use of caesuras. But they will love the way you seem to change from one idea to another on the turn of a sixpence, which is what the caesura gives you the opportunity to do.

I call these lines **changing lines** or **bridging lines**. The first half of the line is the end of the previous thought and the second half is the beginning of the next thought, but it is as yet unfinished. This is a universal pattern. These lines occur regularly throughout the plays; it's essential to immediately recognize them and know how to use them as an acting opportunities.

---

## EXERCISE

### The changing lines

Speak Caliban's line on its own. Practise the change of thought. Engage your brain and embrace the unfinished quality of it with your tone and inflection. It may feel very strange at first. By acknowledging the change of thought in the middle of the line you will naturally take a tiny breath before you move on to the new thought, it is a breath borne of thinking and it is swift. That is not to say that you should ever rush, *speak only as fast as you can think.*

These lines are acting opportunities. Ask yourself why your character is changing thought so abruptly. Just as a change in the iambic dictates an upset in the emotions, the half-lines within the verse structure dictate an upset in your thought patterns; it gives you more to act. I would suggest that Caliban is both vengeful and fearful. This speedy change of thought mid-line gives you the opportunity to explore changing from vengefulness to fearfulness in whatever way you interpret. The technique is universal; the interpretation is yours.

Speak Caliban's next lines using the **thinking breath** and see what acting opportunities you can find within the verse structure. (There are two changing lines.) Move all the way through to the full stop to find the sense of the phrases.

> His spirits hear me,
> And yet I needs must curse. But they'll nor pinch,
> Fright me with urchin-shows, pitch me i' th' mire,
> Nor lead me like a firebrand in the dark
> Out of my way, unless he bid 'em. But
> For every trifle are they set upon me

Alternate between speaking the lines with the thinking breath and speaking them without, so that you really experience the difference for yourself. You would not take a thinking breath at the end of every line in performance, but it is essential to have gone through this stage of finding out where they are.

This way, even after you have dropped some of the thinking breaths, the depth of feeling will stay in your sense memory.

# Paraphrasing

Re-writing the lines in your own words can be very useful, especially when the verse structure is complex. The **paraphrasing** of Caliban's previous six lines would go like this:

> I can be heard but I will swear. I can console myself that the spirits won't hurt me unless Prospero (he) bids them to do so ... but ... they hurt me for every tiny thing I do.

The second last line (a changing line) is typical of Shakespeare's late plays:

> Out of my way, unless he bid 'em. But

The **but** creates a kind of cliffhanger, and is a perfect moment to use the **thinking breath**. Shakespeare's placing of the word **but** is brilliantly human; Caliban takes a breath immediately before the word, marking his change of thought, and then immediately takes a thinking breath after it at the end of the line, as if the thought is almost to painful to express. Shakespeare seems to be telling you when to think and breathe and therefore giving you a specific acting opportunity, which is packed with silent energy. This one tiny word sandwiched between two tiny breaths can reveal an entire universe to the audience: a universe of danger and injustice. Your power as an actor is to be found not just in the words of Shakespeare, but equally in the breaths and silences between the words, wherein the imagination of the audience can be ignited. Debussy's insight that 'Music is the silence between the notes' should also serve as a graceful reminder to the actor.

Some actors find paraphrasing very useful, whilst others do not. If you want to paraphrase a line or phrase so that you have complete clarity for yourself, resist the temptation to abruptly cut from Shakespeare's language to your own and immediately back to Shakespeare. Although this will give you meaning, it will not give you emotional or intellectual engagement.

Begin first by speaking the lines using your own words and ensuring that you use none of Shakespeare's verbs, nouns or adjectives.

Continue to repeat the lines using your own choice of words and phrases, and with each repetition slowly begin to replace your words with Shakespeare's so that for a while you have a glorious mix of invention – yours and his. Take as long as you like to do this, so that you own each of Shakespeare's words as if they are your choice. Some students and actors find this is the best way to connect with the language, whilst others get no pleasure or use from this exercise at all. Try it for yourself to see.

# Doubling

This is the best exercise I know for understanding the power and energy of the thinking breath. It also allows you to experience the detail and intricacies present in the speech. I invented this technique for myself when I was playing Constance in *King John* at the RSC from 2001–2. Constance has extremely lengthy speeches and, toward the end of the long run, I realized I couldn't be sure where the line endings were, so I started doing this exercise for myself when I was warming up. I was beginning to teach Shakespeare to actors and students around this time, so I passed on the technique and it has proved to be popular and useful.

## EXERCISE

[https://vimeo.com/121688486]

It's easy. Speak the whole speech, but say each line twice. If you're holding a script and reading the words, it's best done walking around a room or an empty stage. If you know the speech and don't want to walk around, you can lie down and close your eyes to do it. Try to feel as physically free as you can.

Caliban's speech would go like this:

All the infections that the sun sucks up
All the infections that the sun sucks up

From bogs, fens, flats, on Prosper fall and make him
From bogs, fens, flats, on Prosper fall and make him
By inchmeal a disease! His spirits hear me
By inchmeal a disease! His spirits hear me
And yet I needs must curse. But they'll nor pinch,
And yet I needs must curse. But they'll nor pinch,
Fright me with urchin-shows, pitch me i' th' mire,
Fright me with urchin-shows, pitch me i' th' mire,
Nor lead me like a firebrand in the dark
Nor lead me like a firebrand in the dark
Out of my way, unless he bid 'em. But
Out of my way, unless he bid 'em. But
For every trifle are they set upon me,
For every trifle are they set upon me,
Sometime like apes that mow and chatter at me,
Sometime like apes that mow and chatter at me,
And after bite me, then like hedgehogs which
And after bite me, then like hedgehogs which
Lie tumbling in my barefoot way and mount
Lie tumbling in my barefoot way and mount
Their pricks at my footfall. Sometime am I
Their pricks at my footfall. Sometime am I
All wound with adders who with cloven tongues
All wound with adders who with cloven tongues
Do hiss me into madness. Lo, now, lo!
Do hiss me into madness. Lo, now, lo!
Here comes a spirit of his, and to torment me
Here comes a spirit of his, and to torment me
For bringing wood in slowly. I'll fall flat.
For bringing wood in slowly. I'll fall flat.
Perchance he will not mind me.
Perchance he will not mind me.

The exercise gives you the opportunity to experience how the **thinking breath** at the end of each line gives life and energy to the next line by generating the *need* to speak. Explore the quality and tone of each thinking breath to discover which ones offer you essential acting opportunities. At best this exercise should have the effect of making you crave to speak the speech without the doubling: it is the actor's equivalent to running with weights.

Usually the second reading of the line will be more committed and emotionally charged than the first. This is the one you want to remember. The **changing lines** come into their own, as you get a real sense of how they fit into the speech as a whole. As ever, the vital element for success is to bring your acting to the exercise. Your task is to speak the lines as if they have never been spoken before. You are in essence practising your spontaneity.

When you have been through the speech, doubling all the way through, begin again without the doubling. Use everything you have learnt about the phrasing and the thinking breaths. Once you know a speech well, some of the thinking breaths will naturally fall away, whilst you can use the acting opportunity of others to purposefully reveal thought and feeling.

## EXERCISE

### Last words [https://vimeo.com/121689191]

Speak only the last word of each line. These are the words you drive toward in every line. Learn them as if they were a speech in their own right. These words should be in your inner ear like a chiming bell, reminding you of your potential thinking breath. Once a speech is deep inside your sense memory and some of the thinking breaths have naturally fallen away, their echo should remain and this exercise ensures that they do.

Taken as an abstract poem, these words often distil the inner and outer landscape of character and narrative. Look especially for words that are repeated to give you clues toward your character's

obsessions, Here Caliban's repetition of the word **me** reveals a
level of self-obsession that offers a great starting-point for an
actor.

| | | |
|---|---|---|
| up | but | tongues |
| him | me | lo |
| me | me | me |
| pinch | which | flat |
| mire | mount | me |
| dark | I | |

If you are learning a speech of blank verse, *learn the last words as well*.
Absorb the words as if they were a poem, and know them so that you
can speak them as easily as you can speak your whole speech. Here
are the last words of Hamlet's first soliloquy:

| | | |
|---|---|---|
| melt | mother | uncle |
| dew | heaven | father |
| fix'd | earth | month |
| God | him | tears |
| unprofitable | grown | eyes |
| world | month | post |
| garden | woman | sheets |
| nature | old | good |
| this | body | tongue |
| two | she | |
| this | reason | |

These last words create a perfect distillation of Hamlet's feelings and
narrative, demonstrating how the two are indelibly connected. Use this
exercise to develop your own relationship with the language and essentially take pleasure from your discoveries as you explore the words. Two
last words in the Hamlet speech resonate strongly for me – **reason**
and **eyes** – these are two of Shakespeare's **keywords**, which we will
explore in depth in Part Two.

The rhythm, sound and structure of Shakespeare's words have been analysed over the last chapters in order for you to take ownership of the language and develop a deeper understanding of your craft. However they do not exist in isolation and are, as I have said, inextricably linked together. As you continue from this point in the book, try to recognize and experience how the three elements come together, so that you develop a heightened awareness of the emotional clues and psychological insights hidden within the verse.

# PART TWO

# WORDS, WORDS, WORDS

As an actor, it's vital to discover what drives your character. Shakespeare gives us no character analysis; he gives us only words to speak and from these you have to decipher everything about the person you are playing. It follows that the more obsessive you are about the detail of the words, the more you will discover. Finding acting clues within the rhythm, sound and structure of the language has been the mission of Part One, wherein I have tried to demystify the technical jargon that surrounds Shakespeare's language, but what of the words themselves? The next five chapters tackle the words and show how to begin to put everything together.

# 5
# KEYWORDS

EXERCISES

- Eyes, mind, reason and love
- Using scaffolding with keywords
- Searching for a character's specific keywords

What words should you look for to bring your character to life and to continue the pursuit of Shakespeare's open wound? To begin with the answer lies in four very small ones: **eyes**, **mind**, **reason** and **love**. These four keywords are repeated more than any other in the canon. Shakespeare used these words and their related themes of seeing, thinking and loving to invent a poetic language of humanity, exploring how it *feels* to be alive.

---

**EXERCISE**

Eyes, mind, reason and love
**[https://vimeo.com/121689192]**

To begin, search for the words **eyes**, **mind**, **reason** and **love** and their related verbs: **seeing**, **looking**, **loving**, **thinking** and **knowing**. Make this one of the first things you do when you read a speech and stop when you come to one of them, they will very likely to linked to the others. Here you are at the heart of Shakespeare's poetic

> invention and can begin an investigative task that will bring you
> closer to the inner life of your character. *Speak these phrases as if
> you had just thought of them, as if you had invented the very idea of
> them yourself.*

The next few pages are full of examples. As ever the technique is universal, the interpretative skills are unique. My interpretations are unique to me; use them as a starting-point for your own imaginative perceptions.

# The language of seeing

Here is a speech entirely devoted to the language of seeing and the denial of love. The keywords have been highlighted.

PHOEBE
I would not be thy executioner.
I fly thee, for I would not injure thee.
Thou tell'st me there is murder in mine **eye**.
'Tis pretty, sure, and very probable
That **eyes**, that are the frail'st and softest things,
Who shut their coward gates on atomies,
Should be called tyrants, butchers, murderers.
Now I do frown on thee with all my heart,
And if mine **eyes** can wound, now let them kill thee.
Now counterfeit to swoon, why, now fall down;
Or if thou canst not, O, for shame, for shame,
Lie not, to say mine **eyes** are murderers.
Now show the wound mine **eye** hath made in thee.
Scratch thee but with a pin, and there remains
Some scar of it. Lean upon a rush,
The cicatrice and capable impressure
Thy palm some moment keeps. But now mine **eyes**
Which I have darted at thee, hurt thee not;

Nor I am sure there is no force in **eyes**
That can do hurt.
*As You Like It*, 3.5

Shakespeare's obsession with eyes becomes Phoebe's obsession, which therefore becomes your obsession as you speak the words. By not comprehending the **force of eyes**, Phoebe reveals she has no grasp of love. Shakespeare has used the fundamental connection of seeing and loving to invent a character who doesn't have the imagination to understand love. This is a wonderful comic starting-point, from which she falls head-over-heels in love with Rosalind only minutes later. Of whom she then says:

PHOEBE
           faster than his tongue
did make offence, his **eye** did heal it up.
*As You Like It*, 3.5

Now she is in love herself, she miraculously understands the **force of eyes**.

    Shakespeare invented countless ways that eyes can *move*, all of which you can use as moments of white-hot personal creativity on stage. Toward the end of the speech above, Phoebe says:

              But now mine eyes,
Which I have **darted** at thee, hurt thee not

Speak the line as if it were your invention, as if you have created the idea that eyes can dart. And later in the same play Oliver says:

He **threw** his eye aside
*As You Like It*, 4.2

These numerous ways in which the eyes of Shakespeare *move* are very useful in performance. Be on the look-out for them and bring them to life through gentle emphasis as if your character had thought of it through unique circumstance and personality. Here are two more examples:

IMOGEN
I would have broke mine eye-strings; crack'd them, but
To look upon him, till the diminution
Of space had pointed him sharp as my needle,
Nay, follow'd him, till he had melted from
The smallness of a gnat to air, and then
Have turn'd mine eye and wept.
*Cymbeline*, 1.3

The imagination necessary to invent the idea of possessing eye-strings, which break and crack in order to look upon your departing lover, is a beautiful starting-point from which to explore the depths of Imogen's imagination.

OPHELIA
That done
He seemed to find his way without his eyes,
For out o' doors he went without their help,
And to the last bended their light on me.
*Hamlet*, 2.1

Ophelia's description of Hamlet's eyes bending light upon her is strange and disturbing. Although Ophelia has already had the experience, the coining of the phrase should come to the actor as she says it.

Later in the play, Gertrude has the first-hand experience of Hamlet's 'bending' eye:

GERTRUDE
Alas how is't with you?
That you do bend your eye on vacancy,
And with th'incorporal air do hold discourse?
Forth at your eyes your spirits wildly peep
*Hamlet*, 3.4

Not only can Shakespeare's eyes wound, dart, break, crack and bend light they can also be *exchanged* through first love:

PROSPERO
>At the first sight
They have chang'd eyes.
*The Tempest*, 1.2

This is a perfect example of Shakespeare's connection between eyes and love. As Prospero watches Miranda and Ferdinand fall in love at first sight, he invents the idea that eyes can be instantly exchang'd between two people. It should be a new thought. Perhaps the idea should be as revelatory to him as the experience is to the lovers.

In *A Midsummer Night's Dream*, Bottom has a fair share of the invention of eyes and seeing.

BOTTOM
The eye of man hath not heard, the ear of man hath not seen
*A Midsummer Night's Dream*, 4. 1

PYRAMUS (played by BOTTOM)
I see a voice!
*A Midsummer Night's Dream*, 5.1

PYRAMUS (played by BOTTOM)
But stay, O spite!
But mark, poor knight,
What dreadful dole is here?
Eyes, do you see?
How can it be?
O dainty duck, O dear!
*A Midsummer Night's Dream*, 5.1

Hidden within Bottom's comedy is an exploration of how we see and feel; a great starting-point for the actor, knowing you have the opportunity to balance comedy with depth of feeling. The depths of truth and human experience are often found hidden within the clown's humour.

In *Hamlet*, Shakespeare brings two of his keywords together to create an iconic phrase of the imagination:

HAMLET
My father, methinks I see my father
HORATIO
O where, my lord?
HAMLET
In my mind's eye Horatio.
*Hamlet*, 1.2

This is Shakespeare's invention, spoken from the mouth of Hamlet, and therefore in the moment of speaking it is your fresh invention. I will develop the importance of the **mind's eye** throughout the book. This brilliance is not confined to *Hamlet*. In *All's Well That Ends Well*, Helena defines the imagination as her triple eye, claiming this to be more reliable than her eyesight:

HELENA
Many receipts he gave me, chiefly one
Which, as the dearest issue of his practice,
And of his old experience, th'only darling,
He bad me store up as a triple eye
Safer than mine own two
*All's Well That Ends Well*, 2.1

Helena's grasp of the mind's capacity for vision is equal to that of Hamlet, pointing towards her highly tuned intelligence, a good starting-point for character analysis. This intelligence is at the heart of her wonderfully flawed character; she has the equivalent perceptions of Hamlet and yet has lost her heart to a man fundamentally less imaginative than her.

What the eye sees stays in the mind; the two are inextricably linked. In other words, one's experience of seeing continually changes and expands one's mind. A dynamic way to chart your character's journey is by building a picture of what you see during the course of the play and by doing this you can chart the changes within your character. The intense realization that there is no way back from what you have seen creates the sense of truly being in the moment and therefore keeps your acting in the present.

OPHELIA
> O woe is me,
> To have seen what I have seen, see what I see!
> *Hamlet*, 3.1

Having directly absorbed Hamlet's pain, Ophelia seems to know that she is changed irrevocably. She replaces the past tense of seeing with the present tense, intimating that these new images will stay in her mind's eye. You can use this as a catalyst for what is to come.

Here's Goneril's final line at the end of *King Lear*:

GONERIL
Ask me not what I know.
*King Lear*, 5.3

It suggests that all she has seen will remain locked away as she hurtles toward suicide. Seeing and knowing are inextricably linked.

Similarly these two examples from Macbeth, still using the keywords and themes, show how vision and sight will affect and change a human being:

MACDUFF
Approach the chamber and destroy your sight
With a new Gorgon.
*Macbeth*, 2.3

DOCTOR
My mind she has mated, and amazed my sight.
I think, but dare not speak.
*Macbeth*, 5.1

# The language of loving and thinking

It is almost impossible to separate the four keywords. It is in their connection that you find some of the great starting-points for acting in Shakespeare's plays. *A Midsummer Night's Dream* has a fair monopoly on the language of **love**:

BOTTOM
reason and love keep little company together nowadays
*A Midsummer Night's Dream*, 3.1

Bottom reveals himself to be at the centre of Shakespeare's human inventions. Taken out of context, this line could belong to any of the great Shakespearean lovers. It's very liberating to imagine that characters in Shakespeare's plays are in dialogue with each other. Although you are playing Bottom, this line may make you feel more like Romeo, therefore you can 'think Romeo' as you speak the words. No one will know, we will see and hear Bottom, but you will feel completely different. It's a very potent exercise and one you can experiment with in secret or openly in rehearsal.

And also from *A Midsummer Night's Dream*:

HELENA
Love looks not with the eyes, but with the mind;
And therefore is wing'd Cupid painted blind
*A Midsummer Night's Dream*, 1.1

The four keywords are at the heart of a character's inventiveness, therefore this first line – which packs three keywords together – is literally bursting with fresh realization. This has a direct effect on the way you can deliver the second line; the word **therefore** is a moment of perfect comprehension, alive with new thoughts. These are not recited thoughts; these are mind-blowing thoughts of pure insight, being spoken in the moment they are conceived. By focusing on the revelatory power of the keywords, the character of Helena comes to life and she becomes genuinely funny and likeable rather than knowing and full of self-pity.

In the later plays, Shakespeare's language is often much more compact:

ARVIRAGUS
Love's reason's without reason
*Cymbeline*, 4.2

The young prince's confused feelings for the boy Fidele (who is in fact his sister Imogen) are perfectly expressed by the compacted use of the two keywords. Shakespeare's poetically charged creativity is an opportunity for Arviragus to freshly invent the phrase and thereby discover the confusion of love for himself at the very moment of speaking.

Shakespeare's use of the word **mind**, when placed entirely on its own, is always worth investigating – these moments offer flashes of pure inspiration for the actor to engage with.

HAMLET
To be, or not to be; that is the question:
Whether 'tis nobler in the mind to suffer
The slings and arrows of outrageous fortune,
Or to take arms against a sea of troubles,
And, by opposing, end them.
*Hamlet*, 3.1

LEAR
I fear I am not in my perfect mind.
*King Lear*, 4.7

## EXERCISE

### Using scaffolding with keywords

If a keyword or a related verb is repeated throughout a speech you can use the **scaffolding** exercise to discover the character's thought process and emotional drive. Scan the speech for keywords, or their related verbs, that are repeated more than any other.

This speech depicts the perfect storm between Macbeth's **eyes** and **mind**. I've created a scaffolding around the phrase **I see**:

MACBETH
**Is this a dagger which I see before me,**
The handle toward my hand? Come, let me clutch thee.
I have thee not, and yet **I see thee still**.
Art thou not, fatal vision, sensible

To feeling as to sight? Or art thou but
A dagger of the mind, a false creation
Proceeding from the heat oppressed brain?
**I see thee yet**, in form as palpable
As this which now I draw.
Thou marshall'st me the way that I was going;
And such an instrument I was to use.
Mine eyes are made the fools of the other senses,
Or else worth all the rest: **I see thee still**
*Macbeth*, 2.1

The scaffolding goes like this:

Is this a dagger which I see before me? – I see thee still – I see
thee yet – I see thee still

Speak and repeat these four phrases with a drive toward the last
one; each phrase develops with increased emotional intensity,
creating a climax at the last word. The alliterative use of the **S**
sound creates a quiet claustrophobic atmosphere. Repeat the
scaffolding until it is firmly embedded in your sense memory.
Return to the whole speech. As you speak it out loud, feel how the
emotional drive of the scaffolding is at the centre of the speech,
driving you toward the final phrase and creating a thread of sense
for you to follow.

# Further keywords: Nothing

One of the other words that repeats throughout the canon is the word
**nothing**. It spins through *King Lear* like a tornado, as well as underpinning
the centre of *Macbeth* and *Hamlet*. Shakespeare seemed inspired by the
very thought that there could be 'nothing'. When you see this word, stop
and investigate; it offers a wealth of acting opportunity and inspiration.

Shakespeare was writing his plays when the idea of 'nothing' was new; this was a time of transition. Zero was still a relatively fresh concept; the old method of mathematics, using the traditional roman abacus, and the newly introduced Hindu numerals were both still in use. It was clearly a fundamental word for Shakespeare; therefore allow it to be a fundamental word for you, as though you were inventing it for the first time.

The word **nothing** comes up repeatedly in the next few chapters, proving its significance throughout the plays. Here are a few examples to begin with:

EDGAR
That's something yet. Edgar I nothing am.
*King Lear*, 2.2

As Edgar begins his journey into an abyss of enforced madness and grief, he negates his own name, identifying himself as nothing.

MACBETH
My thought, whose murder yet is but fantastical,
Shakes so my single state of man that function
Is smothered in surmise, and nothing is
But what is not
*Macbeth*, 1.3

Using the connection between thinking and nothingness, Shakespeare expresses the idea that reality and unreality exist as parallels. Macbeth is changed by the ideas as he invents them and speaks them; this is true for so much of the language and you can apply it to your acting throughout the plays. Always be on the lookout for ways to *change the play with your next line*, and equally allow yourself to be changed by speaking the words.

Toward the end of the play, Macbeth's existential understanding has developed into this:

It is a tale
Told by an idiot, full of sound and fury,
Signifying nothing.
*Macbeth*, 5.5

The four **keywords** and their related verbs serve to reveal Shakespeare's obsession with how it feels to be alive and should be a first point of enquiry when looking at your script. Beyond these, Shakespeare gives characters specific keywords of their own; words you repeat more than any other during a speech and indeed during the play. Concentrating on these allows you to get to grips with the specific preoccupations, passions and obsessions of your character. This should be your second point of investigation. It is very likely you will develop your own keywords, which illuminate Shakespeare for you in a personal way.

**Alliteration** can serve its purpose here too; obviously repeated keywords and alliteration are inextricably linked. In Chapter 2 we looked at how **alliterative scaffolding** gives emotional drive and a thread of sense through a section of Hamlet's first soliloquy. The same exercise is now expanded, creating a scaffolding made up of short phrases around repeated words throughout the speech.

---

### EXERCISE

Searching for a character's specific keywords

Scan the speech for words that are repeated more than any other. In Hamlet's soliloquy, the word **month** reveals itself to be repeated four times; this is therefore the specific keyword for the speech. Make a scaffolding of short phrases around the word.

O that this too too solid flesh would melt
Thaw and resolve itself into a dew
Or that the Everlasting had not fix'd
His canon 'gainst self-slaughter; O God, God!
How weary, stale, flat and unprofitable
Seem to me all the uses of this world.
Fie on't, ah fie, fie! 'Tis an unweeded garden
That grows to seed; things rank and gross in nature
Possess it merely. That it should come to this:
**But two months dead:** nay, not so much, not two,

So excellent a king; that was, to this
Hyperion to a satyr; so loving to my mother,
That he might not beteem the winds of heaven
Visit her face too roughly. Heaven and earth
Must I remember? Why, she would hang on him,
As if increase of appetite had grown
By what it fed on; and yet **within a month?**
Let me not think on't: Frailty, thy name is woman.
**A little month**, or ere those shoes were old
With which she follow'd my poor father's body,
Like Niobe, all tears. Why she, even she,
(O Heaven, a beast that wants discourse of reason
Would have mourn'd longer) married with my uncle,
My father's brother; but no more like my father
Than I to Hercules. **Within a month?**
Ere yet the salt of most unrighteous tears
Had left the flushing of her galled eyes,
She married. O most wicked speed, to post
With such dexterity to incestuous sheets!
It is not, nor it cannot come to good:
But break, my heart, for I must hold my tongue.
*Hamlet*, 1.2

The scaffolding of short phrases would go like this:

But two months dead – within a month – a little month – within
a month

Speak and repeat these four phrases with a drive toward the last
one, building toward an emotional climax at the end on the final
word. Each phrase causes Hamlet increased pain. Repeat the
scaffolding until it is firmly embedded in your sense memory.

Use the **brain on/brain off** exercise. Return to the whole
speech. As you speak it out loud, feel how the emotional drive of
the scaffolding is at the centre of the speech, creating a thread of

sense and driving you toward the final **month**. Ensure that you use the scaffolding to enhance the sensation that you are saying these words for the first time.

The plays operate at infinite levels of complexity; embracing politics, religion, class, sexuality, gender and race. However, as an individual actor, it is impossible to portray these huge debates alone: you cannot play the play, you can only play your part. Your task is to understand as deeply as possible how it feels to be you – that is – how it feels to be your character. I have found no better starting-point for this task than to investigate, moment to moment, how your character uses their **eyes** and **mind** to find **reason** and **love**.

# 6
# RHETORIC

We use words to make ourselves understood. The various ways that Shakespeare uses words can be easily recognized. For the most part they are derived from **rhetorical devices**; think of them as different means with which to persuade others that you are right. Within every device is an acting opportunity to make you seem as if you are speaking your thoughts and experiencing changing emotions for the first time in a way that is specifically unique to your character's personality.

## The mind's eye

As introduced in the previous chapter, these two keywords come together to describe the imagination. Shakespeare's language is packed with **metaphor** and **similes**, which you can think of as opportunities to explore the changing images that you see with your character's mind's eye. In Part Three we will take this exploration further, when you are up on your feet, but for now be content to do the following.

---

### EXERCISE

## Images of the mind's eye

When your character uses an image to describe her thoughts and feelings, stop and investigate; try to genuinely see the image in your own mind's eye and experience how that makes you feel. Take the time to close your eyes whilst you speak the words, to investigate the experience of your 'inner seeing'. With each image, there will be new sensations and, in this way, you can build up a changing inner life. At best, your imagination should be crammed with these images, ready to burst out of you at any moment. Crucially they should not be fixed, but rather you should create fresh images each time you re-visit a phrase. The images themselves give you huge clues as to the depth of your character's resourcefulness and the quality of her emotional and intellectual life.

---

Here are some examples. Speak the words and try to see the images at the same time. Only you can see them; this is a chance to build up a secret relationship with your character, which no one can intrude on – equal to that you have with your own mind's eye.

> HELENA
> The air of paradise did fan the house,
> And angels offic'd all
> *All's Well That Ends Well*, 3.2

Helena's exquisite image is worth investigating. Allow yourself to explore images of paradise and angels as you say the words, and experience how it changes your face, voice and body as you do so.

MACBETH
O, full of scorpions is my mind, dear wife!
*Macbeth 3.2*

When Shakespeare uses animals in a mind's eye image, stop and investigate. Allow yourself to feel as if the creature spoken of is taking possession of you as you speak the words. This isn't a mime show – it's a deepening of inner images. It may well be that the word **scorpion** turns your mind's eye to utter blackness or to a disturbing painting by Goya or to the face of your worst enemy. The important element here is to have a response that is particular to you; you don't simply have to see a scorpion.

And continuing with Macbeth:

MACBETH
Approach thou like the rugged Russian bear,
The arm'd rhinoceros, or th'Hyrcan tiger,
Take any shape but that
*Macbeth, 3.4*

# Noticing the verbs and nouns

I have said before that you should always be attempting to change the play with your next line, therefore it's very useful to engage with the precise words you use in order to do so. Look at what the 'doing' words are doing! By emphasizing what the **verbs** are actively doing to the **nouns** and the changes that are being explored within a speech, you will immediately be brought into the present. This exercise can also untangle a seemingly complicated phrase and guide you toward the sense.

## EXERCISE

### Verbs and nouns

Highlight the **verbs** and the **nouns** in the following speech and ask yourself this question: How do the verbs change the nouns?

VIOLA
<u>Make</u> me <u>a</u> <u>willow</u> <u>cabin</u> at your gate
And <u>call</u> upon <u>my</u> <u>soul</u> within the house
<u>Write</u> loyal <u>cantons</u> <u>of</u> <u>contemned</u> <u>love</u>
And <u>sing</u> them loud even in the dead of night.
<u>Halloo</u> <u>your</u> <u>name</u> to the reverberate hills
And <u>make</u> the <u>babbling</u> <u>gossip</u> <u>of</u> <u>the</u> <u>air</u>
<u>Cry</u> out 'Olivia!'
*Twelfth Night,* 1.5

Every line contains a verb acting on a noun. Make two separate scaffoldings of verbs and nouns and speak them out loud, using the **alphabet of emotions** and **alliteration** to find the connections and bring them to life.

<u>VERBS</u>
make, call, write, sing, halloo, make, cry

<u>NOUNS</u>
a willow cabin, my soul, cantons of contemned love, your name, the babbling gossip of the air, Olivia

Repeat the scaffoldings, remembering to increase intensity of emotion as you drive toward the end. In this speech, the pinnacle is the speaking of Olivia's name. By deconstructing the verbs and nouns in this way, it easy to see that Viola's verbs are prosaic and almost monosyllabic, whilst the nouns are romantic and soulful, leading her toward the daring moment of speaking Olivia's name.

Add the two scaffoldings together, concentrating solely on what the verbs are doing to the nouns and practise this out loud:

| | |
|---|---|
| make | a willow cabin |
| call | my soul |
| write | cantons of contemned love |
| sing | cantons of contemned love |
| halloo | your name |
| make | babbling gossip of the air |
| cry | Olivia |

Now return the verbs and nouns to the whole speech and speak it again, ensuring that the verbs actively change the nouns as profoundly as you can, driving the emotional intensity toward Olivia's name.

Here's another example:

OPHELIA
And I, of ladies most deject and wretched,
That **suck'd** the honey of his **music vows**,
Now **see** that noble and most sovereign **reason**
Like sweet bells **jangled**, out of tune and harsh;
That unmatched form and feature of **blown youth**
**Blasted** with ecstasy. O, woe is me,
T' have seen what I have seen, see what I see!
*Hamlet*, 3.1

Make two separate scaffoldings of verbs and nouns and speak them out loud, using the **alphabet of emotions** and **alliteration** to find the connections and bring them to life.

VERBS
suck'd, see, jangled, blasted
NOUNS
music vows, reason, blown youth, ecstasy

Add the two scaffoldings together, concentrating solely and specifically on what the verbs are doing to the nouns.

| suck'd  | music vows  |
| see     | reason      |
| jangled | reason      |
| blasted | blown youth |

Emphasizing the action of the verbs on the nouns will help you pick your way through the sense of this complex speech. Embedded in its centre is Ophelia's connection of **sight** and **reason**, whilst at its culmination is a keyword particular to the play – **ecstasy**.

Once you have understood the thread of sense, you can also use **paraphrasing** – always try to find the most economical way of expressing the language.

And I, of ladies most deject and wretched,
That **sucked** the honey of his **music vows**,

'I have believed the sweet words of Hamlet's love.'

Now **see** that noble and most sovereign **reason**
Like sweet bells **jangled**, out of tune and harsh;
That unmatched form and feature of **blown youth**
**Blasted** with ecstasy

'I immediately **perceive** that Hamlet's **capacity for thought**
has been **rattled**,
his **body** is **ruined** with **frenzied passion**.'

The combination of **now** and **see** at the beginning of the line makes this speech completely active and gives Ophelia the need to speak. The keyword **see** is one of the most dynamic verbs in all of Shakespeare and its emphasis is essential for the sense of the phrase. It is always active and should be spoken as such. Seeing something creates change and therefore moves you and your character forward: *Always stop and carefully work out what your character can see in their mind's eye and therefore what they know as a consequence.* You will change the play every time you say, **I see**.

Give emphasis to the word **now**, it belongs to the group of little words we are about to look at and is always worth exploring.

Return the verbs and nouns to the whole speech and speak it again, ensuring that the verbs actively change the nouns as profoundly as you can.

You'll find that the exploration of verbs and nouns begins to collide intensely with the rhythm, sound, verse structure and keywords. The techniques will now increasingly overlap as we continue looking at ways to bring the language to life.

---

## EXERCISE

### Verbs as 'heart attacks'

When you see a verb at the beginning of a line, stop and investigate. It will very often create a white-hot energy for you to land on and offer a moment of what seems like pure spontaneous thought. I introduced the technique of **heart attacks** in Chapter 1; when the words do not fit the natural iambic, and the rhythm of one heartbeat is reversed, signalling that your character's emotions are jangled. These are very often found at the beginning of verse lines and give emphasis to the meaning and feeling of the phrase.

Shakespeare very often uses a strong sensory verb to create these 'heart attacks', the off-beat rhythm and the active word coming together to make sense of the emotion. Here are some examples:

GHOST
I am thy father's spirit,

**Doomed** for a certain term to walk the night
*Hamlet*, 1.5

IACHIMO
No more; to what end?
Why should I write this down, that's riveted,
**Screwed** to my memory?
*Cymbeline*, 2.2

HELENA
                    but, if yourself,
Whose aged honour cites a virtuous youth,
Did ever, in so true a flame of liking,
**Wish** chastely, and love dearly, that your Dian
Was both herself and love, O then, give pity
*All's Well That Ends Well*, 1.3

LEAR
And let not women's weapons, water drops,
**Stain** my man's cheeks!
*King Lear*, 2.2

CLAUDIUS
            Help angels, make assay
**Bow** stubborn knees, and heart with strings of steel,
Be soft as sinews of the newborn babe.
*Hamlet*, 3.3

# The importance of little words

In Chapter 1 we looked briefly at the power of the words **and** and **all**,
two tiny words that illuminated Hamlet's phrase:

How weary, stale, flat **and** unprofitable
Seem to me **all** the uses of this world.
*Hamlet*, 1.2

Moreover in Chapter 4 the word **but** in Caliban's speech was found to
have an almost hidden power:

unless he bid 'em. **But**
For every trifle are they set upon me
*The Tempest*, 2.2

The little words are always worth investigating, to see if they can
reinvigorate a human quality into a phrase. Remember, these words
should not be over-emphasized at the expense of all others (no word
should be over-emphasized); in fact they serve to highlight other words
and can prove invaluable in making you feel as if you are speaking your
thoughts for the first time.

## EXERCISE

The little words **[https://vimeo.com/121689194]**

When you see a little word on a strong heartbeat, stop and investigate.
Think how it can either change the line or reinvigorate the sense.

Here are some examples. Speak them out loud twice. The first
time do not use any particular emphasis on the highlighted little
word. The second time explore what happens to the line when you
emphasise the little word. This should not be at the expense of the
whole, *an emphasis should always make you feel as if you are going
deeper into the meaning of the line.* See if you can hear and feel the
difference yourself:

CONSTANCE
War! War! No peace! Peace **is** to me a war!
*King John*, 3.1

HAMLET
This **was** your husband. Look you now what follows.
Here **is** your husband
*Hamlet*, 3.4

HAMLET
   Do you see nothing there?
GERTRUDE
Nothing at **all**; yet **all** that **is** I see.
*Hamlet*, 3.4

TITANIA
These are the forgeries of jealousy,
And **never**, since the middle summer's spring,
Met we on hill, in dale, forest, or mead
*A Midsummer Night's Dream*, 2.1

PHOEBE
And **if** mine eyes can wound, now let them kill thee.
*As You Like It*, 3.5

## 'Now': A little word as a heart attack!

If you see the word **now** at the beginning of a line, stop and investigate. Shakespeare uses the device of the **heart attack** to great effect with this little word, the most famous example being the start of Richard III:

RICHARD GLOUCESTER
**Now** is the winter of our discontent
*Richard III*, 1.1

OPHELIA
**Now** see that noble and most sovereign reason
*Hamlet*, 3.1

HAMLET
**Now** might I do it pat, now he is praying.
Hamlet, 3.3

**Now** has the excellent effect of focusing your energy into the present and making whatever you are speaking of seem immediate and present.

# The use of antithesis

Comparing one thing to its opposite, in order to make a point, immediately produces a certain modulation of voice and tone, which makes it seem as if you are making the comparison for the first time. **Antithesis** gives you the opportunity to produce moments of pure thought and invention by balancing your first proposition against your second. It is essential to recognize these comparisons and build them into your character's language to create moments of astuteness. Shakespeare's language is packed with antithesis; use it to bring the intelligence of your character alive and at the same time to deepen your personal interpretative relationship with the character.

## EXERCISE

Antithesis

Look for phrases where characters use comparisons of opposites to make their point. In order to work as a device, antithesis must be bold and definitively compare one extreme to another. So as not to feel like the purveyor of a device, you must engage on a human level with the ideas, which involves engaging your voice with the natural inflection it takes to make comparisons. Here are some examples;

HELENA
Let not **your hate** encounter with **my love**

For loving where you do.
*All's Well That Ends Well*, 1.3

EDGAR
The lowest and most dejected thing of fortune
Stands still in **esperance**, lives not in **fear**.
*King Lear*, 4.1

ROSALIND
I had rather have a **fool to make me merry** than **experience to make me sad**
*As You Like It*, 4.1

LADY MACDUFF
**All is the fear** and **nothing is the love**
*Macbeth*, 4.2

CELIA
When **Nature** hath made a fair creature, may she not by **Fortune** fall into the fire?
*As You Like It*, 1.2

Speak these phrases, committing your mind and voice entirely to making the comparison, ensuring that you are *thinking* about what you are saying. Use the **brain on/brain off** exercise to experience for yourself the mental energy necessary to engage with one simple comparison.

# Word lists

A list of words is a fantastic acting opportunity, it allows you to really seem as if you are thinking on your feet. Countless characters within the plays use lists to make themselves understood. There is a particular modulation of voice that human beings fall into when we deliver a list: rising up as if climbing steps towards the top of a mountain. The last word or phrase we speak would seem to be definitive. Speaking a list of words in a Shakespeare play requires exactly the same inflection as you would use in normal life; it is the spoken equivalent to climbing a mini-mountain.

## EXERCISE

## Lists of words

If you see a list of words or phrases, stop and count the number of steps it takes before you reach the top. Use each word or phrase as a step. I number the steps in my script, so I can pace the journey to the top. Once absorbed into your sense memory, this technique allows feelings to seem as though they are flying. Here's an example:

PAULINA
　　　　　　　(1) A thousand knees,
(2) Ten thousand years together, (3) naked, (4) fasting
Upon a barren mountain, and (5) still winter
In storm perpetual, could not move the gods
To look that way thou wert.
*The Winter's Tale*, 3.2

Paulina's list of words within this speech of raging condemnation has five steps. The first two are short phrases, both using a repeat of the word **thousand**, the next two are one-word condemnations, one has the sound of negativity and the next uses the **F** sound, the greatest sound to swear with. Finally the top of the list is a longer phrase, with which she reaches the 'top of the mountain' and finally makes her point.

> The audience do not want to hear a list, and nor should they, but they do want to see Paulina fly with rage at Leontes. This technique will allow you to do just that. The technique is universal, the way you use it is completely personal and unique.

Shakespeare also uses lists to great comic effect:

ROSALIND
I saw her hand: she has a (1) leathern hand,
A (2) freestone-colour'd hand; I verily did think
That (3) her old gloves were on, but 'twas her hands:
She (4) has a huswife's hand; but that's no matter.
*As You Like It*, 4.3

The structure of the list adds comic value to the words. It seems to me the third step of the list is the 'top of the mountain' and the fourth and final step is more of a throwaway line.

The longer the list, the more incensed and motivated the character may be. This technique of dealing with lists is very useful, as you may one day have to say this:

KENT
(1) A knave; (2) a rascal; (3) an eater of broken meats; a base, proud, shallow, beggarly, three-suited, hundred-pound, filthy, worsted-stocking (4) knave; a lily-liver'd, action-taking knave, a whoreson, glass-gazing, super-serviceable, finical (5) rogue; one-trunk-inheriting (6) slave; one that wouldst be a bawd in way of good service, and art nothing but the composition of a (7) knave, (8) beggar, (9) coward, (10) pander, and the son and heir of a mongrel (11) bitch; one whom I will beat into clamorous whining, if thou deniest the least syllable of thy addition.
*King Lear*, 2.2

Kent is climbing several mountains of rage in this speech; one list of insults immediately follows another. Instead of numbering every word,

I've numbered the different stages, each ending with a definitive name or noun and yet still climbing, reaching the top of the mountain with the mongrel bitch. This, in itself, creates a small scaffolding of names, which you can use to get to grips with the structure of the speech.

knave – rascal – eater of broken meats – knave – rogue – slave – knave – beggar – coward – pander – mongrel bitch

This example shows how the different techniques and exercises begin to work together to bring the language to life. The speech is in prose, which we are about to look at in the next chapter, but the same notion of driving through to the end of the punctuation remains, so that the sense of the phrase is intact.

# The use of puns

## EXERCISE

### Puns

If there is more than one obvious meaning to a word, stop and investigate; Shakespeare's use of puns is prolific and offers various acting opportunities. These are entirely dependent on the nature of the play and the context with which they are spoken. The language of Shakespeare's clowns is packed with puns and many of them full of sexual innuendo. The word **nothing**, for example, has multiple connotations, not least as a name for female genitalia – which can be quite literally translated as 'no thing'. That is not to say that every time the word 'nothing' is spoken it is making that specific reference – context is everything where puns are concerned.

It is essential to remember that it is not only the clowns who use puns in their language. I would suggest that Hamlet is doing so when he repeats the word back to Ophelia in this exchange after the nunnery scene.

HAMLET
Lady shall I lie in your lap?
OPHELIA
No, my lord.
HAMLET
I mean, my head upon your lap?
OPHELIA
Ay, my lord.
HAMLET
Do you think I meant country matters?
OPHELIA
I think nothing, my lord.
HAMLET
That's a fair thought to lie between maids' legs.
OPHELIA
What is, my lord?
HAMLET
Nothing.
*Hamlet*, 3.2

A pun often works in this way; the first character – Ophelia – speaks the word with one meaning and the second character – Hamlet – speaks it with an entirely different connotation, providing a wealth of acting opportunity, as they perceive how the meaning has changed.

In this next example Hamlet uses a pun on the word 'sun' to gain ground over his uncle:

CLAUDIUS
How is it that the clouds still hang on you?
HAMLET
Not so, my lord, I am too much i' the sun.
GERTRUDE
Good Hamlet, cast thy nighted colour off
*Hamlet*, 1.2

Hamlet's superficial answer uses the **sun** in response to the **clouds** of Claudius's question, however sun and son sound exactly the same. Hamlet's deeper answer – his other meaning – seems to be implying, 'I remain the son of the dead king, your brother', and it manages to silence Claudius. The next person to speak is Gertrude; Hamlet's use of provocative punning provides all three characters with psychological insight and an intense acting opportunity.

# 7
# PROSE AND VERSE

EXERCISES

- Deciphering the prose
- Sharing the language

Coleridge's description of the serpent twisting and untwisting its own strength is as apposite for the prose as it is for verse. Shakespeare's language expresses our patterns of thought, which are always moving forward; changing and developing in order to communicate our feelings and desires. This is equally true for soliloquys and dialogue, verse and prose. The structure of blank verse serves to support these patterns, and creates the illusion that characters are speaking 'naturally'. Both *Hamlet* and *King Lear* have long sections of prose, immediately dispelling the myth that prose is reserved only for the working people of the plays. It is however true that Shakespeare's clowns favour the prose over the verse.

When speaking in prose, the absence of the verse structure gives you the chance to appear to grapple with your feelings and thoughts, as if they are harder to express. This does not however give you the chance to add your own pauses and punctuation. Most of the techniques you have learnt so far can be applied to the prose, in order for you to bring your character to life and explore the open wound. Prose can be thought of as 'verse trying to escape'.

## EXERCISE

Deciphering the prose

The crazed ramblings of Lear on the heath are written in prose:

> Look, look, a mouse! Peace, peace; this piece of toasted cheese
> will do 't. There's my gauntlet, I'll prove it on a giant. Bring
> up the brown bills. O, well flown, bird: I' th' clout, i' th' clout!
> Hewgh! Give the word.
> *King Lear*, 4.5

Move from one major punctuation mark to the next to get the sense
of the phrase. Depending on what you find, use the techniques
already set out for the verse to bring the phrase to life. The only
technique that won't apply is the thinking breath at the end of a
verse line. Remember the punctuation will vary from one edition to
another; do not panic, if there are discrepancies between editions,
simply use your intelligence to make a choice as to where you feel
the phrase comes to an end.

**Look, look,** a mouse!

Stop straight away. The word **look** belongs to the four keywords and
their related verbs. It belongs to **eyes** and **seeing**. This word should
immediately tell you to stop and investigate, doubly so, as here it
is immediately repeated. Lear is in the centre of Shakespeare's
invention and therefore immediate detective work should be taken.
What is he looking at? Is there a mouse? Is he seeing it in his
mind's eye? Who is he talking to? Himself? Edgar? The audience?
Any good actor will ask all these questions and more, but knowing
where the keywords are within a huge role is essential in order to
give emphasis to certain moments. As ever, the technique part is
universal; your answers will be unique.

Additionally, the **alliteration** of these first two words gives immediate speed of thought and creates a natural heartbeat rhythm. *We only repeat things in life in order to be understood better, therefore, if two words are repeated next to each other, always give a little more emphasis to the second one.* Furthermore the **alphabet of emotions** gives you a collision between the sound of **love** and the **mother** sound.

Although Lear is not speaking in blank verse, after only four words, a pattern of sound and rhythm which illuminates his thoughts and feelings can be found.

Let's move on:

**Peace, peace**; this **piece** of toasted cheese will do 't.

The triple **alliteration** (which includes a **pun**) gives immediate speed of thought and creates another natural heartbeat rhythm. *Once more, be sure to give slightly more emphasis the second time you say it.* Now you can investigate whether there is any iambic rhythm within the line.

My natural emphasis would be as follows:

<u>Peace</u>, <u>peace</u>; this <u>piece</u> of <u>toast</u>ed <u>cheese</u> will <u>do</u> 't.

The first two words are equally spaced, with a naturally stronger emphasis on the second word. The rest of the line has a perfect iambic rhythm; the great king on the heath feeding cheese to a mouse (whether real or imaginary), appears like a gemstone of iambic within the mud of the prose. You should have no expectation of how the heartbeats will fit into the rhythm of the prose, but it is always useful to experiment and sometimes a line will appear, as this one does, reminding you that prose is 'verse trying to escape'; the prose is indeed very close to the verse.

There follow eight very short phrases, which would mainly seem to be commands, creating an echo of the king's past life:

There's my gauntlet. I'll prove it on a giant. Bring up the brown
bills. O, well flown, bird: I' th' clout, i' th' clout! Hewgh! Give the
word.

I would use two different techniques. First apply the **verbs and
nouns** exercise and then look at the **alliteration**. You can create a
**scaffolding** for each:

VERBS
prove
bring
flown
give

NOUNS
giant
brown bills
bird
word

Add the two scaffoldings together, concentrating solely on what the
verbs are doing to the nouns:

prove giant
bring brown bills
flown bird
give word

This is almost the whole speech, as if his language at this point has
been pared down to its bare requirements; there is no fuss. Perhaps
this is a direct consequence of his transformative experience in the
storm, perhaps his weakness prohibits him from making long florid
sentences, perhaps, like a child, he is enjoying the simplicity of the
words. All these are personal interpretative thoughts that come from
the universal technical exercise of deconstructing the language.

Now return the verbs and nouns to the whole speech and speak it again, ensuring that the verbs actively change the nouns as profoundly as they can.

# Blank verse

In *As You Like It,* Jaques makes direct reference to speaking in blank verse, as opposed to prose. Rosalind and Jaques are speaking in prose, when Orlando enters, he speaks one line of perfect iambic. Jaques immediately comments on this, as if Orlando is a dullard and that his blank verse could not be as interesting as Jaques' own prose. And so he leaves. Rosalind, however, continues the scene in prose.

Look for the **keywords** and the **little words**, the **alliteration**, the **antithesis** and the **alphabet of emotions** to bring the scene to life. The construction of the first speech contains a long list. I have highlighted some techniques and left many for you to find for yourselves. Have a look at the journey of the words **sadness** and **sad**, which are shared by Jaques and Rosalind, and then changed into **happiness** by Orlando.

JAQUES
I have neither the scholar's melancholy, which is emulation; nor the musician's, which is fantastical; nor the courtier's, which is proud; nor the soldier's, which is ambitious; nor the lawyer's, which is politic; nor the lady's, which is nice; nor the lover's, which is **all** these, but it is a melancholy of mine own, compounded of many simples, extracted from many objects, and indeed the sundry contemplation of my travels, in which my often rumination wraps me in a most humorous **sadness**.
ROSALIND
A traveller. By my faith, you have great **reason** to be **sad**. I fear you have sold your own lands **to see** other men's. Then to have **seen** much and to have **nothing** is to have rich **eyes** and poor hands.
JAQUES
Yes, I have gained my experience.

ROSALIND
And your experience makes you **sad**. I had rather have a **fool to make me merry** than **experience to make me sad** — and to travel for it, too.

*Enter ORLANDO*

ORLANDO
Good **day** and **happiness, dear** Rosalind.
JAQUES
Nay then, God be wi' you, an you talk in blank verse.
ROSALIND
Farewell, Monsieur Traveller.
*As You Like It*, 4.1

Jaques' direct comment on blank verse highlights the constant push and pull between verse and prose, which itself highlights an essential Shakespearean acting skill; to remain simultaneously inside and outside of the play, 100 per cent psychologically true to your character and 100 per cent aware that you are performing on stage. This may be true of all acting, but it is vital for Shakespeare, otherwise it would be impossible to turn to the audience and share your thoughts.

Just as every human being is at the centre of their own lives, every character believes that they are the centre of the play. If your character is speaking in prose, a second actor may attempt to 'pull the play away from you' by speaking in verse and returning the play back onto the heartbeat rhythm. This push and pull adds an underlying muscularity to the scenes, whether comic or tragic, and adds something extra to the alert listening of the actors.

The heath scene in *King Lear* is a good example. It begins with Lear speaking in prose. Gloucester's first line is in verse, as if he is trying to pull Lear into his play and his world, but without success; Lear continues in prose. Then Gloucester tries again and this time Lear joins him and is pulled out of his solitude and into dialogue. Whether or not this was purposeful from Shakespeare, or an unconscious mistake, or indeed the heart of his mysterious genius we will never know – what's vital is that the actors can use it to deepen their relationship with the language and with the experience of acting on stage with each other.

This push and pull between prose and verse runs true through the plays.

GLOUCESTER
I know that voice.
LEAR
Ha! Goneril, with a white beard! They flattered me like a dog; and told me I had white hairs in my beard ere the black ones were there. To say 'ay' and 'no' to every thing that I said! 'Ay' and 'no' too was no good divinity. When the rain came to wet me once, and the wind to make me chatter; when the thunder would not peace at my bidding; there I found 'em, there I smelt 'em out. Go to, they are not men o' their words: they told me I was everything; 'tis a lie, I am not ague-proof.
GLOUCESTER
The trick of that voice I do well remember:
Is 't not the King?
LEAR
Ay, every inch a king:
When I do stare, see how the subject quakes.
I pardon that man's life.
*King Lear*, 4.5

In order to 'pull Lear back into the verse', the two men share a verse line; the five heartbeats of one line of iambic is split between the two characters. The iambic is the rhythm of your character's feelings; therefore sharing the iambic is an intimate sharing of feeling.

## EXERCISE

### Sharing the language

Characters often **share the same word** in a densely packed pattern. Stop if you see this on the page and investigate. This sharing of words shows that the characters are bound intimately together. A close investigation of the specific words that are shared will give you further interpretative acting opportunities. Both characters may share a word but they will have completely different attitudes toward that word, for example:

**GLOUCESTER**
Is 't not the King?
**LEAR**
Ay, every inch a king.

Shared verse lines offer a sense of intimacy between two characters; the more closely they share the verse, the more connected they are, whether they like it or not. This is a famous example from *King John*, in which the King is persuading Hubert to murder the young prince Arthur.

KING JOHN
Death.
HUBERT
My lord?
KING JOHN
A grave.
HUBERT
He shall not live.
KING JOHN
Enough.
*King John*, 3.3

The single words they share within one line of verse create a bond between them. In this case, they agree to the murder of a child without having to explicitly say the words. Here are two more examples; the shared words are highlighted:

GHOST

Revenge his foul and most unnatural **murder**
HAMLET
**Murder?**
GHOST

**Murder** most foul, as in the best it is.
But this most foul, strange and unnatural.
*Hamlet*, 1.5

The sharing of the word **murder** (made from the **mother** sound) creates a moment of intimacy moment between the father and son. For me, this shared intimacy marks the exact point at which the Ghost's poison is metaphorically passed on to Hamlet.

LEAR
Speak.
CORDELIA
**Nothing**, my lord.
LEAR
**Nothing?**
CORDELIA
**Nothing**.
LEAR
How? **Nothing** can come of **nothing**. Speak again.
*King Lear*, 1.1

Lear and Cordelia share the keyword **nothing** at the beginning of the play, creating an intimate bond of tragic consequence between them. The word **nothing** is the fulcrum on which the play turns and becomes a keyword for each of the protagonists throughout the course of the play. The technique, in this case investigating **shared words** is, as ever, universal, whilst the interpretations will always be personal and unique to whoever is in the room working on the play.

# 8
# PUTTING IT ALL TOGETHER: SOLILOQUYS

In the next two chapters we'll take soliloquys and scenes, to show how to use the techniques and exercises to begin to bring the language to life. Rather than pinpoint everything on every line, I move through the speeches from phrase to phrase, with different examples of how to combine the techniques to achieve spontaneity. The objective is to begin to recognize the patterns in the language for yourself and develop an ownership of the words, so that your unique interpretative thoughts and feelings can be released by the universal techniques.

## What is a soliloquy?

A soliloquy is an articulation of your thoughts and feelings that cannot – and must not – be shared with any other character in the play. It's essential that in the moments before you begin to speak, you should feel as if you are about explode with the frustration of not being able to express yourself. Take the time to explore the inherent danger that would be incurred if you shared these thoughts and feelings with anyone else, in order to engage with your character's *need* to speak in solitude.

Once speaking, think of the soliloquy as a 'conversation of my thoughts' in which you battle with yourself in order to find a solution to a problem. To be very plain – in the beginning there is a situation which forces you to speak, in the middle you reach a crossroads or a crisis and by the end you reach a solution; of sorts. It is essential to beware of self-pity; never fall into the trap of telling the audience of your woes, but rather approach a soliloquy as if you are searching for meaning, in order to actively find a solution to your predicament – there is no room for self-pity in these plays.

Whether or not you directly share the language with the audience as if confiding in them, or play the speech as an internal monologue, thereby inviting the audience to bear witness to your inner world, is entirely down to preference and dependent on the nature of the production. But however you play it, the essential key is your *need* to speak, and thereby your need for change; a soliloquy is a speech during which you undergo some level of transformation, not only in terms of the narrative of the play, but in your depth of feeling and experience.

In *All's Well That Ends Well*, Helena is compelled to speak, having read Bertram's letter of rejection, which she quotes at the beginning of the speech. Scan the soliloquy and see which techniques and exercises jump out at you first. Take pleasure in the way the different elements of language collide.

HELENA
'Till I have no wife, I have nothing in France.'
Nothing in France, until he has no wife!
Thou shalt have none, Roussillion, none in France;
Then hast thou all again. Poor lord! Is't I
That chase thee from thy country and expose
Those tender limbs of thine to the event
Of the none-sparing war? And is it I
That drive thee from the sportive court, where thou
Wast shot at with fair eyes, to be the mark
Of smoky muskets? O you leaden messengers
That ride upon the violent speed of fire,
Fly with false aim; move the still-peering air,
That sings with piercing; do not touch my lord.
Whoever shoots at him, I set him there;
Whoever charges on his forward breast,
I am the caitiff that do hold him to't;

And, though I kill him not, I am the cause
His death was so effected: better 'twere
I met the ravin lion when he roar'd
With sharp constraint of hunger; better 'twere
That all the miseries which nature owes
Were mine at once. No, come thou home, Roussillon,
Whence honour but of danger wins a scar,
As oft it loses all: I will be gone;
My being here it is that holds thee hence:
Shall I stay here to do't? No, no, although
The air of paradise did fan the house
And angels offic'd all: I will be gone,
That pitiful rumour may report my flight,
To consolate thine ear. Come, night; end, day!
For with the dark, poor thief, I'll steal away.
*All's Well That Ends Well*, 3.2

The first phrase is a perfect storm of alliteration, keywords and antithesis. The alliteration of **France, nothing, none** and **wife** give Helena speed of thought, which drives her toward the little word **all,** which is used in antithesis to the word **nothing**, which together with the word **none** creates the **alliterative scaffolding** of the whole phrase – Shakespeare is on fire and therefore so is Helena:

'Till I have no **wife**, I have **nothing** in **France**'.
**Nothing** in **France**, until he has no **wife!**
Thou shalt have **none**, Roussillon, **none** in **France**;
Then hast thou **all** again.

This is a middle/late play and the structure is complex. There are many **changing lines** and therefore the sense of the speech is often left unfinished at the end of the verse lines. Make a **last word** list of the next three phrases, to place the **thinking breaths** in your sense memory. These lists are particularly useful when the structure of verse is complex.

I
expose

event

I

thou

mark

messengers

fire

air

lord

The list reveals the close alliteration on the **mother** sound and the antithesis between **fire** and **air**. It also reveals a connection between herself **– I** – and Bertram – **thou, lord.**

Now try the **doubling** exercise on this same section. This will give you an opportunity to hear and feel the various techniques in combination with each other and allow you to practise them in your own time. This exercise always highlights where the changing lines are and gives you the chance to practise them, discovering for yourself when Helena's mind makes a dynamic change of thought, allowing you to find your thread of sense through the speech. To remind you: the first half of the line is the end of the previous thought and the second half is the beginning of the next thought, but it is as yet unfinished. The changing lines in this section are:

Then hast though all again. Poor lord! Is't I

Of the none-sparing war? And is it I

Of smoky muskets? O you leaden messengers

Now speak this section again without the doubling. Before you leave this section, look at the following line – it is a perfect example of a verb as **heart attack**:

Fly with false aim; move the still-peering air

**Fly** is the first word; a verb at the beginning of a line, which immediately creates the **mini heart attack**. This rhythm is combined with the **F** sound, which connects alliteratively with the next off-beat: **false.** The jangled rhythm continues through the line, confirming that Helena's emotions are rocked. This concurs completely with her mind's eye images of Bertram on the battlefield, surrounded by the bullets, which narrowly miss him at her command.

Now the structure and rhythm change and become very simple, allowing Helena to conclude her sense at the end of the lines. This is the beginning of her 'crisis point', wherein she sees into the truth and simultaneously her imagination begins to take flight. Look at how the **alphabet of emotions** and the **alliteration** – highlighted here – support her thought process as she takes the blame for him going to war:

> Whoever **sh**oots at him, I set him there;
> Whoever charges on his **f**orward breast,
> I am the **c**aitiff that do hold him to't;
> And though I **k**ill him **n**ot, I am the **c**ause
> His **d**eath was so e**ff**ected

Her collision of sound perfectly mirrors her inner turmoil; she uses the greatest sound to **swear** with and the second greatest sound to swear with. These collide with the sounds of **killing** and **negativity** which lead to the sound of **death**.

Helena's words perfectly fit the rhythm of the iambic, showing her to be in the centre of her emotions – her natural state is revealed as that of a woman who can imagine her lover's death and take responsibility for it. She has reached the crisis point, at which she has imagined the death of Bertram. Her **mind's eye** knows no bounds, as she creates an image of herself in the clutches of the ravin hungry lion. This gives birth to the idea of all the world's misery belonging to her; a perfect example of Coleridge's serpent twisting and untwisting its own strength:

> better 'twere
> I met the **ravin** lion when he **roar'd**
> With sharp constraint of hunger; better 'twere
> That **all** the miseries which nature owes
> Were **mine** at once.

The alliteration of the **R** sound creates a roaring lion. Emphasizing the little words of **all** and **mine** gives sense to her feelings and creates a feeling of spontaneity.

Now she comes to her decision:

> No, come thou home, Roussillon,
> Whence honour but of danger wins a scar,
> As oft it loses all: I will be gone;
> My being here it is that holds thee hence:
> Shall I stay here to do't? No, no, although
> The air of paradise did fan the house
> And angels offic'd all: I will be gone,
> That pitiful rumour may report my flight,
> To consolate thine ear. Come, night; end, day!
> For with the dark, poor thief, I'll steal away.

Twice she repeats the four-word phrase, **I will be gone**, which fundamentally changes the play. Make these into a scaffolding:

> I will be gone – I will be gone

Repeat them, so that the first time you say the phrase it is sensitive and new, almost like a fresh sensory experience; an idea not yet resolved upon. The second time, speak these same words with resolve and conviction. The strength of the iambic rhythm underpins this acting opportunity.

Return the words to the speech, incorporating your acting into the language. The repetition of this four-word phrase creates a structure in the middle of which is Helena's most beautiful mind's eye image:

> The air of paradise did fan the house
> And angels offic'd all:

Speak this phrase and find the pictures in your mind's eye. Return it to the speech and try to find the pictures each time you speak these words; they are your acting secret.

There is no reason to overemphasize the rhyme of the last two lines, they provide a gentle means of pulling the speech together.

Practise the different sections, so that you know which techniques you are aiming for in each one. You can of course use all the techniques throughout the speech and should experiment for yourself as to which exercises make the most sense for you and give you the greatest feelings of freedom and liberty within the language. I would always recommend trying the **doubling** exercise and the **last word** exercise for every speech of blank verse.

# Prose soliloquys

Gloucester is on stage with Edmund. The speech can be spoken to Edmund or taken as a soliloquy to the audience, turning back to Edmund when he speaks to him at the end. It has the distinct feel of a soliloquy, as Gloucester has a problem at the beginning, which leads to a crisis, out of which he makes a very clear and distinct decision. Scan the speech and see what jumps out at you first:

> GLOUCESTER
> These late eclipses in the sun and moon portend no good to us; though the wisdom of nature can reason it thus and thus, yet nature finds itself scourg'd by the sequent effects. Love cools, friendship falls off, brothers divide. In cities, mutinies; in countries, discord; in palaces, treason; and the bond crack'd 'twixt son and father. This villain of mine comes under the prediction; there's son against father: the King falls from bias of nature; there's father against child. We have seen the best of our time. Machinations, hollowness, treachery, and all ruinous disorders follow us disquietly to our graves. Find out this villain, Edmund; it shall lose thee nothing; do it carefully. And the noble and true-hearted Kent banish'd! His offence, honesty! 'Tis strange.
> *King Lear*, 1.2

Take one full phrase at a time by moving toward the major punctuation marks. The first phrase is made of two sentences:

> These late eclipses in the sun and moon portend no good to us; though the wisdom of nature can reason it thus and thus, yet nature finds itself scourg'd by the sequent effects.

Look at the first sentence. The words fit the rhythm of the iambic; it lasts for eight full heartbeats:

These <u>late</u> ec<u>lip</u>ses <u>in</u> the <u>sun</u> and <u>moon</u> por<u>tend</u> no <u>good</u> to <u>us</u>

Gloucester is in the centre of his emotions and able to cope with these bad signs in the universe, but then the rhythm collapses into prose, signalling that it is impossible for him to keep thoughts and emotions in check. Remember, the prose gives you the chance to appear to grapple with your feelings and thoughts, as if they are harder to express.

The second sentence brings us to a deeper understanding of how the plays use **keywords** to bind family members together. Nature and fortune are key themes throughout the plays; they are very often repeated and used in antithesis with each other. Each play reveals its own keywords, to which characters have their personal and particular relationship. In *King Lear* one of those words is **nothing** and another is **nature.** At the beginning of the scene, unknown to Gloucester, Edmund has begun his soliloquy:

Thou, nature, art my goddess. To thy law
My services are bound.

We have looked at the power of **sharing words** and the intimacy this reveals between characters speaking to each other on stage. Here we begin to see how the keywords resonate for the audience by the completely different way that the characters use them. At the beginning of his soliloquy, Edmund speaks of nature as a lawful goddess whom he wishes to reject, as she has deemed him an unworthy bastard, but at the beginning of this soliloquy, Gloucester sees nature as being ruined by the events revealed to him.

It is essential to know not only what the language means for yourself and your character, but also how the words you speak go toward creating the entire panorama of the play.

The sentence uses a subtle **antithesis**, within which Gloucester balances the reliable wisdom of nature against the punishing reality of nature's fate. Where there is antithesis, use your natural vocal inflection to bring the thought processes to life. This natural inflection will immediately give colour to your voice, making you recognizably human.

The next two phrases are a perfect example of **verbs acting on nouns**. They barely need to be made into scaffoldings. The lack of grammar around the words creates an almost visionary effect:

> Love cools, friendship falls off, brothers divide. In cities, mutinies; in countries, discord; in palaces, treason; and the bond crack'd 'twixt son and father.

And now the visionary experience develops as Gloucester's **mind's eye** takes over. Speak the next phrase to yourself, ensuring that you create a secret visual story depicting the fall of fathers, sons and kings:

> This villain of mine comes under the prediction; there's son against father: the King falls from bias of nature; there's father against child. We have seen the best of our time.

These mind's eye images lead Gloucester to his key phrase: '*We have seen the best of our time.*' It's important, because crucially it contains what he has **seen**. Stop and investigate this, it is the heart of Shakespeare's invention and therefore the heart of Gloucester's invention. On investigation the line contains the whole play, literally for Gloucester; within days he will be blind.

Of course he doesn't know this and it would be hideous to do some ridiculous acting that signalled this in any way. But it gives you something crucial on your journey through the play – it gives you active hindsight. Later in the play, once Gloucester has been blinded and the truth of Edmund's foulness has been revealed to him, he will naturally think back to this early encounter. As an actor on stage, if you have already committed wholly to speaking that line with innocence – '*We have seen the best of our time*' – you will have planted a memory for yourself and you can use it to berate yourself. I describe this as **laying down a marker** for yourself, leaving a trail of emotionally and intellectually committed moments in the first half of a play, to which you can return in order to deepen your inner life as you experience the story developing in the second.

The next phrase requires you to make a **list** – I've numbered the steps up to the 'top of the mountain':

> (1) Machinations, (2) hollowness, (3) treachery, and **all** (4) ruinous disorders follow us disquietly to our graves. Find out this villain, Edmund; it shall lose thee nothing; do it carefully. And the noble and true-hearted Kent banish'd! His offence, honesty! 'Tis strange.

Use your natural vocal inflection to ensure that you sound as if you are speaking your thoughts for the first time. The **dis** in front of the word **quietly** is very useful and characterful if you speak it as if you were inventing the idea that **quiet** could be changed to its opposite just by saying **dis** in front of it.

Finally Gloucester takes action and gives Edmund a direct command, unknowingly falling straight into his trap. Contained within the command is one of the keywords of the play – the potency of which we looked at in Chapter 5 – **nothing**. Stop and investigate it. From there the final phrases can serve as further opportunity to lay down markers to use with hindsight later in the play. The more you commit to them at the moment you speak them, the more potent they will be for you in the latter stages.

As with the verse, practise the different sections of the speech, concentrating on using the specific techniques from above. Be sure that each phrase *makes sense* before you put them all together. Create **scaffoldings** of your own, using **alliteration**, **keywords** and **sound patterns** to create the effect of complete spontaneity. Finally remember the idea of Coleridge's serpent, twisting and untwisting its own strength to ensure that one thought leads inexorably to the next and the images created by your mind's eye are deeply and unalterably connected to each other.

Finally let's take Hamlet's first soliloquy, adding further analysis to the work we've already done with it. His words, feelings and ideas are far too dangerous to be shared with anyone in the play; his grief is deep and intimate – giving rise to the soliloquy.

O that this too too solid flesh would melt
Thaw and resolve itself into a dew
Or that the Everlasting had not fix'd
His canon 'gainst self-slaughter. O God, God!
How weary, stale, flat and unprofitable
Seem to me all the uses of this world.
Fie on't, ah fie, fie! 'Tis an unweeded garden
That grows to seed; things rank and gross in nature
Possess it merely. That it should come to this:
But two months dead: nay, not so much, not two,
So excellent a king; that was, to this
Hyperion to a satyr; so loving to my mother,

That he might not beteem the winds of heaven
Visit her face too roughly. Heaven and earth
Must I remember? Why, she would hang on him,
As if increase of appetite had grown
By what it fed on; and yet within a month?
Let me not think on't: Frailty, thy name is woman.
A little month, or ere those shoes were old
With which she follow'd my poor father's body,
Like Niobe, all tears. Why she, even she,
(O Heaven, a beast that wants discourse of reason
Would have mourn'd longer) married with my uncle,
My father's brother; but no more like my father
Than I to Hercules. Within a month?
Ere yet the salt of most unrighteous tears
Had left the flushing of her galled eyes,
She married. O most wicked speed, to post
With such dexterity to incestuous sheets!
It is not, nor it cannot come to good:
But break, my heart, for I must hold my tongue.
*Hamlet*, 1.2

Rhythmically the first three lines begin with **mini heart attacks**, which immediately reveal Hamlet's heartbroken inner life, as if he can't begin speaking without pain. There is a close sound pattern between **O**, **thaw** and **or**, which reflects and underpins the sound of heartbreak. Emphasizing the little word **or** provides focus to the **antithesis** that underpins the whole phrase: between Hamlet's initial desire to melt away into dew and his frustration at God's prohibition of suicide. The phrase ends with his repetition of the word **God**, which is against the rhythm, again causing his heart to split and further reflect his jangled feelings:

**O** that this too too solid flesh would **melt**
**Thaw** and resolve itself into a **dew**
**Or** that the Everlasting had not **fix'd**
His canon 'gainst self-slaughter. O God, **God**!

There is an absence of obvious alliteration in this phrase, as if Hamlet is slowly chipping this antithesis from the ice of his mind, which has the effect of highlighting the sounds of the words at the ends of the lines – the **mother** sound, the sound of **death**, the greatest sound to **swear** with, followed by the word **God**.

The next phrase invokes images of a desperate world and a garden of strangulation – commit to these in your mind's eye, to feel the effect of Hamlet's psyche. Although motivated by personal experience, the images he conjures remain universal, as if to keep his own story at arm's length. The abstracted emotional territory is reflected by the simple structure; there are no changing lines.

> How weary, stale, flat and unprofitable,
> Seem to me all the uses of this world.
> Fie on't, ah fie, fie! 'Tis an unweeded garden,
> That grows to seed; things rank and gross in nature
> Possess it merely.

This abstraction changes with the first **changing line** of the speech, as if his frustration bursts out of him:

> Possess it merely. That it should come to this

From here on he is in dialogue with himself and in the very next line chastises himself, with a short attack of **alliteration** – using the sound of negativity – for not getting the facts exactly right:

> But two months dead**: nay, not so much, not two,**

Now look at the intertwined connection between the structure of the language and the outpouring of Hamlet's imaginative life, as the speech continues with a series of his intimate **mind's eye** images, reflected by the complex structure of continuous **changing lines**. Focus on using the **thinking breath** to create the feeling of spontaneity as the unstoppable force of his imagination takes hold. Try the **doubling** exercise on the speech from here up to the end.

He sees his father protecting his mother's cheek from a gust of wind, his mother embracing his father as if she would never let him go, his mother in new shoes weeping as she follows his father's coffin, his mother's marriage to his uncle, his mother's raw flushed-out eyes and finally his uncle and his mother copulating between incestuous sheets. Embracing these **mind's eye** images and seeing them for yourself is an essential task of playing Hamlet and speaking this speech.

The kaleidoscope of images is punctuated by Hamlet asking himself if he can bear to see them, if he can bear to remember. '*Must I remember?*' becomes an intensely resonant phrase when, in a few scenes time, the ghost of his father asks him to '*Remember me*'. If you commit to seeing these images as you speak them – actively remembering them as you speak them – you will have **laid down a marker** for Hamlet's next soliloquy when he says:

> Remember thee?
> Yea, from the table of my memory
> I'll wipe away all trivial fond records
> *Hamlet*, 1.5

The intense grief he feels in this speech is rendered merely trivial in a few pages' time.

Thinking of a soliloquy as the **conversation of my thoughts** and deconstructing the arguments within the conversation is a fundamental technique for unlocking the energy within the speech. Divide the speech into two voices, using everything that he sees in his mind's eye as one voice and everything that frames the images as the other.

First select the phrases that provide the framework.

But two months dead: nay, not so much, not two

Heaven and earth
Must I remember

and yet, within a month
Let me not think on't

Frailty, thy name is woman
A little month

Why she, even she

Within a month:

It is not, nor it cannot come to good:
But break, my heart, for I must hold my tongue.

Contained in these short pithy phrases is the thread of Hamlet's obsession with the alliterative keyword – **month** – that we highlighted back in Chapter 5. '*Must I remember*' and '*Let me not think on't*' suggest that Hamlet is not in control of the unconscious images that beset him, he is in fact in conversation with them or indeed battling against them.

Now look at the construction of the images themselves, within which I've highlighted three keywords.

So excellent a king; that was, to this
Hyperion to a satyr; so **loving** to my mother,
That he might not beteem the winds of heaven
Visit her face too roughly.

Why, she would hang on him,
As if increase of appetite had grown
By what it fed on

or ere those shoes were old
With which she follow'd my poor father's body,
Like Niobe, all tears.

O Heaven, a beast that wants discourse of **reason**
Would have mourn'd longer

married with my uncle,
My father's brother, but no more like my father
Than I to Hercules.

Ere yet the salt of most unrighteous tears
Had left the flushing of her **galled eyes,**
She married.

O most wicked speed, to post
With such dexterity to incestuous sheets!

Spoken on their own, the images are striking, but have no natural flow. It is only when they are placed within the short phrases that reveal Hamlet's inner battle that they make sense. Put the two halves together, making sure that you know where the **battle points** are and how the speech works as a **conversation**.

Toward the end of the speech the **alliteration, alphabet of emotions, keywords** and **rhythm** collide as Hamlet crystallizes his precise inner demon – the fresh marriage of his mother.

Why **sh**e, even **sh**e
(O Heaven, a beast that wants discourse of reason
Would have **mourn'd** longer) **married** with my uncle,
**My** father's brother, but no **more** like **my** father
Than I to Hercules: within a **month**?
Ere yet the salt of most unrighteous tears
Had left the flushing of her galled eyes,
**She married.**

The repetition of the swearing **she** at the beginning of the phrase creates a densely packed alliterative pattern, telling you that Hamlet's brain is on fire at the very thought of Gertrude. The repetition of the **mother** sound throughout this section builds to a storming conclusion when Hamlet finally allows himself to speak these words:

**She married.**

Rhythmically the two words present a **mini heart attack** – a moment of heartbreak, where both beats are naturally emphasized and the rhythm of Hamlet's feelings is completely rocked. This resonates with the swearing **sh** sound that has already been set up a few lines before and culminates with the **mother** sound that has been building through the speech and reaches its apotheosis here. There is a desperate sadness with which Hamlet uses and repeats the **mother** sound – the warmest sound he can make – when it is his mother's actions that have caused him so much grief.

Follow the patterns of **alliteration** to find the contrast between the fire and ice of Hamlet's temperature. The keywords come into play here. There is an absence of alliteration in the first line and it ends with a keyword, **reason**, prompting you to speak it as if it is borne out of you slowly – you are at the heart of Shakespeare's invention. The next phrase can be spoken with more pace and energy, prompted by the alliteration on the **mother** sound and culminates with the word **month**.

This is followed by another image, free from alliteration and once more ending with a keyword – **eyes**. Here the heart of Shakespeare's invention is Hamlet's 'close-up' vision of his mother's eyes: raw, red and bitter. This is the image that he carries into the moment at which he can utter the words that seem to kill his heart:

**She married**.

This specific image of her eyes leads to the image of incestuous copulation, from which Hamlet makes the decision to repress his feelings with his broken-hearted vow of silence on the last line of the speech, which we looked at in Chapter 1.

# 9
# PUTTING IT ALL TOGETHER: SCENES

In this chapter we'll look at two scenes, one in verse and the other prose. As you read them, continue to see how much of the rhythm, sound, structure, keywords and rhetoric are immediately visible to you and use the techniques and exercises to begin to make your own connections with the language.

## Verse

The plots of Shakespeare's plays can only be revealed through the words that the characters speak. Although soliloquys serve to reveal the narrative, the majority of the storytelling is achieved by the characters' talking to each other, using words. As I've said many times, all you have is the words. Here is an early scene from *Twelfth Night*, containing much exposition. We'll use the techniques to explore how character and spontaneity is embedded within the language, however much plotting there may seem to be on the surface.

Scan the scene and see what jumps out at you first:

VIOLA
What country (friends) is this?
CAPTAIN
This is Illyria, lady.
VIOLA
And what should I do in Illyria?
My brother he is in Elysium.

Perchance he is not drown'd: what think you, sailors?
CAPTAIN
It is perchance that you yourself were saved.
VIOLA
O my poor brother! and so perchance may he be.
CAPTAIN
True, madam: and, to comfort you with chance,
Assure yourself, after our ship did split,
When you and those poor number saved with you
Hung on our driving boat, I saw your brother,
Most provident in peril, bind himself
(Courage and hope both teaching him the practice)
To a strong mast that lived upon the sea;
Where, like Arion on the dolphin's back,
I saw him hold acquaintance with the waves
So long as I could see.
VIOLA
For saying so, there's gold:
Mine own escape unfoldeth to my hope,
Whereto thy speech serves for authority,
The like of him. Know'st thou this country?
CAPTAIN
Ay, madam, well; for I was bred and born
Not three hours' travel from this very place.
VIOLA
Who governs here?
CAPTAIN
A noble duke, in nature as in name.
VIOLA
What is the name?
CAPTAIN
Orsino.
VIOLA
Orsino! I have heard my father name him:
He was a bachelor then.
CAPTAIN
And so is now, or was so very late;
For but a month ago I went from hence,

And then 'twas fresh in murmur, (as, you know,
What great ones do the less will prattle of)
That he did seek the love of fair Olivia.
VIOLA
What's she?
CAPTAIN
A virtuous maid, the daughter of a count
That died some twelvemonth since, then leaving her
In the protection of his son, her brother,
Who shortly also died: for whose dear love,
They say, she hath abjured the company
And sight of men.
*Twelfth Night*, 1.2

Start by looking at the first exchange and thinking about what they have just been through. The two of them have experienced a near-death experience out at sea, indeed the captain suggests that he may have saved her life; he has certainly witnessed her being saved from drowning. This creates a bond between them that is immediately reflected in the way they share their language; I have highlighted the **shared words** and the **keywords**. I have also highlighted how much love there is between them at the beginning of the scene through the simple repetition of the sound of **love**:

VIOLA
What country (friends) is this?
CAPTAIN
This is Illyria, lady.
VIOLA
And what should I do in Illyria?
My brother he is in Elysium.
**Perchance** he is not drown'd: what **think** you, sailors?
CAPTAIN
It is **perchance** that you yourself were saved.
VIOLA
O my poor brother! and so **perchance** may he be.
CAPTAIN
True, madam: and, to comfort you with **chance**,

Assure yourself, after our ship did split,
When you and those poor number saved with you
Hung on our driving boat, **I saw** your brother,
Most provident in peril, bind himself
(Courage and hope both teaching him the practice)
To a strong mast that lived upon the sea;
Where, like Arion on the dolphin's back,
**I saw** him hold acquaintance with the waves
**So long as I could see**.

The intimacy of their near-death experience is revealed through their close sharing of the words **perchance** and **chance**. The words themselves convey the precariousness of their circumstance and indeed of life.

Create a **scaffolding** of the shared words and share it between *two* actors:

VIOLA
perchance
CAPTAIN
perchance
VIOLA
perchance
CAPTAIN
chance

It is actually a mini version of the conversation and can be used as such, the first two words being almost a question and answer. The third **perchance** seems to have Viola's doubt infused through it, which makes the captain's answer of **chance** more definitive, bringing the exchange to a close. As with all scaffoldings, it should be played so that there is an emotional drive toward that last word. Act the scene using these four words. Return the scaffolding to the lines and let the dynamic of the scaffolding create a conversation between the two actors.

Now look at the captain's speech, which would seem to be solely exposition; however there is always something within the language that will reveal character. Concentrating on the keywords and key theme of what the captain saw (highlighted) brings the character into the centre of the play and demonstrates why he *needs* to speak beyond telling the audience the story.

Make a scaffolding of the three phrases:

I saw – I saw – so long as I could see

Repeat this scaffolding, creating the emotional drive through to its end. (It does by chance create a perfect line of iambic.) Concentrate on the *need* to say these two words – **I saw**. He needs to say it to persuade Viola that her brother is alive. He needs to say it to console her, to give her reason to live. But simultaneously he needs to say it because it was an extraordinary sight and he needs to share his experience. As we've said before, one's experience of seeing has the effect of continually changing and expanding one's mind. Perhaps we can understand human experience as this – **we see**, **we know**, **we tell**.

With this in mind, return to the speech, incorporating the scaffolding to infuse the speech with the personal need to speak.

Let's look at the next section between the two of them. It's useful, in an exchange of short lines like this, to speak the lines of each character separately and then put them back into their conversational pattern.

Let's take Viola first:

VIOLA
For saying so, there's gold:
Mine own escape unfoldeth to my hope,
Whereto thy speech serves for authority,
The like of him. **Know'st thou this country?**

**Who governs here?**

**What is the name?**

Orsino! I have heard my father name him

Question, question, question! Now the captain:

CAPTAIN
**Ay, madam, well; for I was bred and born**
**Not three hours' travel from this very place**.

**A noble duke, in nature as in name**.

**Orsino.**

Answer, answer, answer!

Where **questions and answers** come thick and fast, stop and investigate. Commit with your whole soul to asking a question – you must genuinely need to know the answer.

The exposition is unfolding *because* of Viola's questioning curiosity, which comes from her need to survive on her own. The captain has an affection for Viola borne out of their near-death experience; he is forthcoming, kind and a self-confessed gossip (by his own revelation), so the answers come thick and fast. These would be my initial interpretations; as ever, the feelings are personal, and the technique of investigating questions and answers is universal.

As the scene continues the gossip unfolds:

VIOLA
Orsino! I have heard my father name him:
He was a bachelor then.
CAPTAIN
And so is now, or was so very late;
For but a month ago I went from hence,
And then 'twas fresh in murmur (as, you know,
What great ones do the less will prattle of)
That he did seek the love of fair Olivia.

The rhythm of the verse is perfect iambic, the words fitting the rhythm easily; he is at the centre of his emotions, comfortable with the gossip. The speech contains some lines in brackets. If you see **brackets** on the page, stop and investigate. A humanizing – though not essential – acting technique is to use the brackets to laugh your way *through* the line. (If you have a copy of the first folio, the placing of the brackets is extremely reliable.) This is a subtle art; I am by no means suggesting that you laugh uproariously at what you have said, adding extra '*hahas*' to the rhythm, but rather that the laughter affects the way you speak and breathe as you deepen your response to what you are saying. This technique gives you the chance to express a self-reflecting irony that fires off all sorts of echoes in your mind. It works as well for the tragedies, as it is does for the comedies.

There are three examples in this scene.

VIOLA
What country (friends) is this?

Viola has experienced a near-death experience; my instinct is that she is crying with the relief of being alive and grief for her presumably dead brother – her laughter through the word **friends** allows her to express her gratitude to the sailors and thankfulness for her very life.

CAPTAIN
I saw your brother,
Most provident in peril, bind himself,
(Courage and hope both teaching him the practice)
To a strong mast that lived upon the sea

In the captain's speech, the brackets take up a whole line, offering him a world of acting opportunity as he comments on Sebastian's character, before going back to his main course of thought. '*Courage and hope*' would echo strongly with a man of the sea; the laughter through this line could have a melancholic flavour, tinged with the memory of past ship-wrecks.

And the third pair of brackets:

CAPTAIN
For but a month ago I went from hence,
And then 'twas fresh in murmur (as, you know,
What great ones do the less will prattle of)
That he did seek the love of fair Olivia.

And here his laughter is one of pure self-deprecation. He confesses to his 'prattling', which makes sense of the scene and allows him to unfold more gossip in his next speech.

Obviously you can laugh through a line at any point in the plays, and in performance you may find these moments of natural irony develop on their own. However as a starting-point I have found this technique, of using the brackets, to be effective, psychologically true and reliably specific.

In the captain's final speech of this section, the structure of his verse has completely changed:

VIOLA
What's she?
CAPTAIN
A virtuous maid, the daughter of a count
That died some twelvemonth since, then leaving her
In the protection of his son, her brother,
Who shortly also died: for whose dear **love**,
They say, she hath abjured the company
And **sight of men**.

In his previous speech, which was light-hearted in content, he spoke with a very simple verse structure. Now that he is delving more deeply into the tragedy of the double death and Olivia's self-imposed solitary life, it is much harder for him to articulate. This is directly reflected in the structure of the verse, which is entirely made of changing lines, each one finishing without yet concluding the sense until the last line of the phrase. This structure brilliantly reflects the captain's difficulties in articulating the tragic events. Use the **doubling** system here to practise this more complex structure.

I've also highlighted the two keywords to show the continued connection between **love** and **sight** within the language. Practise each short section on its own, ensuring that each actor knows what the other is doing. It is helpful to use the exercise of one actor speaking all their lines without interruption, followed by the second actor doing the same, so that each is aware of 'their part'. This will heighten the quality of listening between the two when you put the scene back together. The vital issue of **listening** is something we will now begin to explore.

Shakespeare often returned to themes in his plays and whole speeches are revisited and reused. In *The Tempest*, written approximately ten years after *Twelfth Night*, Francisco tells the lords how he saw Ferdinand save himself from drowning in the storm:

FRANCISCO
Sir, he may live:
**I saw** him beat the surges under him,
And ride upon their backs; he trod the water,
Whose enmity he flung aside, and breasted
The surge most swoll'n that met him; his bold head
'Bove the contentious waves he kept, and oar'd
Himself with his good arms in lusty stroke
To the shore, that o'er his wave-worn basis bow'd,
As stooping to relieve him: **I not doubt**
**He came alive to land**.
*The Tempest*, 2.1

The structure of the speech is fundamentally more complicated than the captain's, although packed with the changing lines and jangled rhythms of the later plays, the similarity is striking. However, the phrase **I saw**, which connects with the last line (highlighted above), remains Shakespeare's key for the actor to create the need to speak. After ten years, his obsession with the connections between **seeing** and **knowing** remained present and alive.

# Prose

The prose often looks more unfathomable on the page than the verse. Move from phrase to phrase and apply the techniques slowly; it is not as different from verse as it looks. Read through the scene to see how much of the rhythm, sound and structure are immediately visible to you, and use the techniques and exercises to begin to make your own connections with the language.

Rosalind has the vast majority of words to speak in the following scene, so what does Orlando do? He listens. As a rule we only speak when someone listens to us and, in order to keep them listening, we have to invent fresh ways of inventing our words. In Shakespeare this requires that the listeners *really* listen. I call it **active listening**, because the listener must have an *active need* to hear the words that are being spoken. Equally the speaker must have an *active need* to be heard. Throughout this scene, Orlando *needs* to listen as much as Rosalind *needs* to speak. This *mutual need* to speak and listen is essential for Shakespeare's language to live.

Scan the scene and see what jumps out at you first. To begin, look for any shared words or phrases that create an intimacy between the two characters. I've highlighted the most obvious one, a sharing of the phrases **I am he** and **are you he**, which creates a mini version of the scene.

ORLANDO
Can you remember any of the principal evils that he laid to the charge of women?
ROSALIND
There were none principal; they were all like one another as half-pence are, every one fault seeming monstrous till his fellow fault came to match it.
ORLANDO
I prithee, recount some of them.
ROSALIND
No, I will not cast away my physic but on those that are sick. There is a man haunts the forest, that abuses our young plants with carving 'Rosalind' on their barks; hangs odes upon hawthorns and elegies on brambles; all, forsooth, deifying the name of Rosalind: if I could meet that fancy-monger, I would give him some good counsel, for he seems to have the quotidian of love upon him.
ORLANDO
**I am he** that is so love-shaked: I pray you, tell me your remedy.
ROSALIND
There is none of my uncle's marks upon you: he taught me how to know a man in love; in which cage of rushes I am sure you are not prisoner.
ORLANDO
What were his marks?

ROSALIND

A lean cheek, which you have not; a blue eye and sunken, which you have not; an unquestionable spirit, which you have not; a beard neglected, which you have not; but I pardon you for that, for simply your having in beard is a younger brother's revenue: then your hose should be ungartered, your bonnet unbanded, your sleeve unbuttoned, your shoe untied and everything about you demonstrating a careless desolation; but you are no such man; you are rather point-device in your accoutrements, as loving yourself than seeming the lover of any other.

ORLANDO

Fair youth, I would I could make thee believe I love.

ROSALIND

Me believe it! you may as soon make her that you love believe it; which, I warrant, she is apter to do than to confess she does: that is one of the points in the which women still give the lie to their consciences. But, in good sooth, **are you he** that hangs the verses on the trees, wherein Rosalind is so admired?

ORLANDO

I swear to thee, youth, by the white hand of Rosalind, **I am that he, that unfortunate he**.

ROSALIND

But are you so much in love as your rhymes speak?

ORLANDO

Neither rhyme nor reason can express how much.

*As You Like It*, 3.2

Here's the **shared scaffolding**:

ORLANDO
I am he
ROSALIND
are you he?
ORLANDO
I am that he – that unfortunate he.

Share the scaffolding between two actors, ensuring that the natural inflection of the conversation is stored in your sense memories. Try different ways of playing this scaffolding, from the very tentative to the very bold and almost everything in-between.

Return the scaffolding to the full scene, ensuring that the vocal inflection and feeling of the conversation remains in your voices when you speak these words – they really create a scaffolding on which the scene rests. There is a sizeable gap between Orlando's **I am he** and Rosalind's **are you he**. You can use this discovery to great advantage here. Perhaps she can't bring herself to ask him the question, because she is too overwhelmed by her own feelings, or perhaps she is toying with him for as long as she likes, before landing on the direct question. The scaffolding technique is universal and gives you a solid thread of sense, though the interpretative choices are infinite.

Now use the technique of looking at what one character says without the other. Always begin with the person who says the least. Use the universal techniques to look for patterns in the language with which to emphasize thought and emotion. In a prose section such as this, you are also looking for hidden lines of verse.

ORLANDO
Can you remember any of the principal evils that he laid to the charge of women?

I prithee, recount some of them.

**I am he** that is so **love-shaked**: I pray you, tell me your remedy.

What were his marks?

Fair youth, I would I could make thee believe **I love.**

I swear to thee, youth, by the white hand of Rosalind, **I am that he, that unfortunate he**.

Neither **rhyme nor reason** can express how much.

Orlando asks only two questions and, with the exception of the second line, he is repeatedly attempting to persuade Rosalind of his identity. Spoken as one speech, these seven lines create their own crescendo, as if the whole thing were a scaffolding inside Rosalind's language, culminating with one of Shakespeare's **keywords – reason**. I've highlighted the keywords, which create a pattern, telling you where Orlando is at his most inventive. In this instance his inventiveness leads him to create the idea that one can be **shaken by love**. Use the **sh** sound – the second greatest sound to swear with – to create a specific attitude toward the phrase. Is Orlando delighted to be shaken by love, or is he appalled by it? The interpretative feelings are yours; the technique of stopping and investigating keywords and phrases is universal.

Now take a look at this line:

I would I could make thee believe I love.

It has an iambic rhythm running through it. Although the words don't quite fit to the rhythm – there's a **mini heart attack** in the centre of the line, reflecting Orlando's jangled emotions – there is enough iambic to make it stand out in the middle of Rosalind's prose, as if Orlando is trying to pull the play back into blank verse, a battle he sorely loses.

Now look back at the text, reading only Rosalind's words, taken on their own. Her first phrase is a direct answer to Orlando's question. Their sharing of the word **principal** catches their intimacy.

ORLANDO
Can you remember any of the **principal** evils that he laid to the charge of women?
ROSALIND
There were none **principal**; they were **all** like one another as half-pence are, every **one fault** seeming monstrous till **his fellow fault** came to match it.

The **antithesis** between **one fault** and **his fellow fault** creates the colourful inflection of voice that makes Rosalind seem as if she is speaking her thoughts as she is making them up. The little word **all** is – as always – very useful to emphasize, and the **F** sound, the greatest sound to swear with, can be investigated. She is not, of course, swearing directly at Orlando, but the effect of the repetition of the sound reveals her inner energy.

Now take a look at the next speech:

No, I will not cast away my physic but on those that are sick. There is a man haunts the forest, that abuses our young plants with carving 'Rosalind' on their barks; hangs odes upon hawthorns and elegies on brambles, all, forsooth, deifying the name of Rosalind: if I could meet that fancy-monger I would give him some good counsel, for he seems to have the quotidian of love upon him.

The technique of thinking through to the end of a line in order to find the sense is essential.

No, I will not cast away my physic but on those that *are* **sick**.

This first short phrase needs driving through to the end so that the idea of **sickness** is clearly invented and established; for the rest of the speech Rosalind riffs around this theme.

Now use the **verbs and nouns** technique. Make two separate scaffoldings of verbs and nouns and speak them out loud, using the alphabet of emotions and alliteration to find the connections and bring them to life.

VERBS
haunts, abuses, hangs, deifying, meet, give

NOUNS
forest, young plants, odes, name of Rosalind, fancy monger, good counsel

Speak the scaffoldings out loud. The **alphabet of emotions** is strong – the sound of **breath** and whispers colliding with the sound of **death** followed by the **mother** sound. The alliteration of **haunts** and **hangs** creates a whispered intimate effect.

Add the two scaffoldings together, concentrating solely on what the verbs are doing to the nouns and practise this out loud. The connection of **haunt** and **forest** creates a fleeting ghost-like figure, which can generate intense **mind's eye** images for Rosalind as she speaks and Orlando as he listens. (We will explore how to share mind's eye images in Part Three.)

| | |
|---|---|
| haunts | forest |
| abuses | young plants |
| hangs | odes |
| deifying | name of Rosalind |
| meet | fancy monger |
| give | good counsel |

Now return the verbs and nouns to the whole speech and speak it again, ensuring that the verbs actively change the nouns as profoundly as you can.

Look at this last line:

for he seems to have the quotidian of love upon him.

It poses a common conundrum. The word **quotidian** is not often in use in nowadays and the audience is unlikely to understand its meaning. If you don't understand a word, look it up in a reliable Shakespearean dictionary (for example, D. and B. Crystal, *Shakespeare's Words*. London: Penguin, 2004). A quick check will reveal that **quotidian** means a fever that comes on once a day.

If you see a word you don't understand, stop and look it up. Absorb the word into your own intellect as if you yourself had freshly invented that word to fit the meaning. Then, using the techniques of rhythm, sound and structure, your task is to make sure the audience understands the sense, if not the specific meaning.

The next long speech takes the form of a list. I've numbered the script so that technically you can see the 'steps to the top of the mountain'. The interesting question is why does she make the list so long? To which the answer must lie in the fact that she *needs* him to listen; the longer the list, the longer he will wait for her to reach the pinnacle and the longer he waits, the longer she has him in her presence. It's a pretty clever device. There are two 'mountains' to climb:

(1) A lean cheek, which you have not, (2) a blue eye and sunken, which you have not, (3) an unquestionable spirit, which you have not, (4) a beard neglected, which you have not; but I pardon you for that, for simply your having in beard is a younger brother's revenue:

then your (1) hose should be ungartered, your (2) bonnet unbanded, your (3) sleeve unbuttoned, your (4) shoe untied and (5) **everything** about you demonstrating a careless desolation; but you are no such man; you are rather point-device in your accoutrements, as loving yourself than seeming the lover of any other.

The word **everything** – highlighted here – is the pinnacle of the list. It has the same effect as the word **all** and, although not particularly small, you can add it into your list of little words to look out for throughout the plays.

Let's look at Rosalind's final speech in this section:

Me **believe it!** you may as soon make her that you love **believe it**; which, I warrant, she is apter to **do** than to confess she **does**: that is one of the points in the which women still give the lie to their consciences. **But**, in good sooth, **are you he** that hangs the verses on the trees, wherein Rosalind is so admired?

Everything here is leading toward the line that contains the all-important scaffolding: **are you he**? Follow the alliteration to discover her speed of thought. The first phrase is linked by the alliterative repetition of **b**'s and **d**'s which gives this phrase some speed of thought. The alliterative **believes** lead the ear to the word **but** later on in the speech.

Now look at this central line of discovery:

**that is one of the points in the which women still give the lie to their consciences**

It has less alliteration running through it, just one densely compacted clash of **which** and **women** that gives her the opportunity to have a boiling-hot attitude toward the word women. The rest of the line can be spoken slowly as if the words are being borne out of Rosalind less easily and she is in fact discovering something for herself. This is a fantastic starting-point. If she appears already to know everything about men and women she will be a nag and a bore. One of the essential keys to playing her is that she discovers the complexities that exist between the sexes for herself, as she reveals them to Orlando, speaking her thoughts for the first time. Following the alliteration in this moment allows her time to slowly discover this complex revelation for herself in the moment of speaking.

Finally let's look at her last line:

But are you so much in love as your rhymes speak?

This simple and monosyllabic line would benefit from an investigation into the sounds you are making. The **alphabet of emotions** gives you the **mother** sound colliding with the sound of **love**. In addition to this, try the vowels in isolation on this line. Her depth of feeling for him is overwhelming, but she can't tell him, as she must stay in disguise. This exercise allows you to discover the inner soul of the line.

u ... ah ... ooo ... oh ... u ... i ... u-ah ... a ... or ... eye ... eee?

Use the **brain on/brain off** technique to ensure that your thoughts and feelings are fully engaged with the sound. Begin very slowly and repeat the pattern, gradually increasing speed without losing the connection with thought.

Return to speaking the words with vowels and consonants together, maintaining your newly discovered soulfulness within the apparent casual delivery of Ganymede – Rosalind's *alter ego*.

# Essential reminders for putting it all together

The more you know about the construction of the language, the freer you will be when you are up on your feet.

## *Rhythm*

- The **detective of emotions** exercise does not change the way you deliver a line – it deepens your understanding of your inner life.
- Natural rhythm does not mean neutral feelings. You are always feeling something.

- An inversion or a trochee is a **mini heart attack** – a moment of potential heartbreak or ecstatic happiness.

## Sound

- **Alliteration** can be understood as the temperature and speed of your thoughts.
- Where alliteration is densely packed, it is as though your brain is on fire. Where it is sparse or absent, your thoughts are borne slower out of you, as if chipped out of ice.

## Alphabet of emotions

- The consonants have as much feeling embedded in them as the vowels. Ignore them at your peril.

## Structure: When to breathe

- The structure of the verse is like a serpent, twisting and untwisting its own strength. It is unstoppable.

## Keywords

- Stop and investigate the play every time you see **eyes**, **mind**, **reason** and **love** or their related verbs. You will be at the heart of Shakespeare's poetic invention.
- Change the play with your next line!

## Rhetoric

- **Rhetoric** is a multifarious means of persuading others you are right.
- Sometimes the life of a phrase will be revealed through emphasizing the little words – **and**, **all**, **if** and **but**.

## Prose

- The prose is 'verse trying to get out'.

- Characters try to pull each other from prose to verse and vice versa in order to be at the centre of the play.

To share the discoveries of drama students, see: [https://vimeo.com/121689195].

# A last word: Committing to *'me'*

When using personal pronouns, bring your understanding of yourself to the centre of your investigation and allow the ideas to resonate inside you. It matters not whether the words **me**, **mine** or **myself** are emphasized – what matters is the personal connection you make to the experience of saying them.

Some examples:

HAMLET
How all occasions do inform against me
*Hamlet*, 4.4

CALIBAN
This island's mine, by Sycorax my mother,
Which thou tak'st from me.
*The Tempest*, 1.2

CONSTANCE
I am not mad, this hair I tear is mine
*King John*, 3.4

CALIBAN
For every trifle are they set upon me
*The Tempest*, 2.2

No one other than oneself understands how it feels to say the word **me**. To put it another way: *'Only I know what it's like to be me'*. Bring yourself to your acting – let it be personal. The audience will see and hear Hamlet, Caliban or Constance, whilst you are engaging with the experience of being alive. The degree to which you do this is entirely up to you, but it will make the difference between being good and being completely unforgettable. It will also make acting and directing these plays purposeful and fulfilling, no matter who is performing them or who is making up the audience.

# PART THREE

# GAMES TO PLAY IN REHEARSAL

The exercises in Parts One and Two have concentrated on how to gain ownership of the language through a detailed analysis of the words on the page. These words are all you have to begin with and therefore reading them must be your point of entry. I've emphasized how important it is to 'act' during the all these exercises; bringing your heart and feelings to the language as you practise is essential. However, as an actor, you have more than your sentient voice, you have a body with which to express yourself and through which you will bring your character to life. Therefore in order to discover how the language can truly affect you it is essential to be up on your feet.

The techniques and exercises in the third section of this book are best played as games facilitated by a teacher in a workshop or director in rehearsal. Create an acting space, set out with a semi-circle of chairs, so that the actors can join the space easily. For the purpose of clarity, I will set the games out addressing the facilitator.

All games can be modified and used as starting-points for creativity. If you are not involved in rehearsal or workshop, these exercises are still useful to read through and adapt for your own means.

PART THREE

GAMES TO PLAY
IN REHEARSAL

# 10
# GAMES OF THE MIND'S EYE: SOLILOQUYS

EXERCISES

- Chain of creativity
- The impulse to speak
- Prompting
- Exploding the mind's eye images

## Chain of creativity

[https://vimeo.com/121689196]
[https://vimeo.com/121689947]

The first exercise should be played with a group of actors immediately after you have worked on a speech using the techniques in Parts One and Two. It is essential that the words are fresh in the actors' minds in order for the exercise to work. The fundamental idea is to allow the actors freedom to explore how it feels to play their character, unhampered by having to look down at a script in their hands. I will use Hamlet's first soliloquy, which you should now be familiar with:

> O that this too too solid flesh would melt
> Thaw and dissolve itself into a dew
> *Hamlet*, 1.2

## EXERCISE

The actors play in partners; one is the 'sculptor' and the other the 'model' or the ' human clay'. Before starting you should establish that both actors are happy to make physical contact with each other. Without speaking and with complete silence in the room, the sculptor moulds her partner into a still image of Hamlet at the moment before he speaks, allowing her recent understanding of the speech to inform her creative instincts. As the 'clay', her partner is compliant and allows herself to be placed in any position; she may be curled up in a ball, leaning against a wall or slumped in a corner, whatever the sculptor desires. The only rule is that the partners must stay in the room. It is essential for the sculptor not to 'think' too hard, but to respond impulsively to the words she has been immersed in; with this in mind, the process should take as long as feels natural. In order to define facial expression, the sculptor can demonstrate the desired expression with her own face for the model to copy.

Once the sculptor has created an image she is happy with, she moves away from the model, who remains in the position, keeping as still as she can. The image now belongs to the model and the chain of creativity can begin. The experience of being moulded in this way allows the model to feel sensations resulting from the specific physicality she has been given; therefore she will already begin to be engaged with feeling and thought before she speaks the words.

The sculptor now makes a series of slow handclaps in order to 'bring the model to life'. At each handclap the model makes one movement with her body, as if slowly moving forward in time and exploring how Hamlet may physically exist. She then waits in her new position for the next handclap – it is as if she is responding to a pause/play button. These movements should not be large or demonstrative; the model is not attempting to *show* Hamlet to an audience, but rather to explore how it may feel to *be* Hamlet.

> After four or five handclaps, the sculptor makes a double handclap and the model reverses the movements she has made in one smooth action, until she lands back at her original picture.

Swap partners, so that each actor can experience the different roles. Bring more partners up from the group and encourage everyone to explore their creativity. Emphasize that you do not need to be 'clever' to achieve this exercise, you need to be in touch with your innate feelings.

You can have everyone up on their feet working with partners, or allow time for the group to watch each partnership. If you are working with a group all day, this is an extremely useful exercise to play in the afternoon – having absorbed the text using the techniques from Part One in the morning. It has the effect of allowing actors 'to play' and reminding them that their response to Shakespeare is unique and valid, whatever their level of experience.

When everyone has created a model, the actors can spread out around the room and take their starting positions. Lead them through a series of handclaps in order let them begin to explore their physicality and then allow them all to come to life naturalistically, whispering the soliloquy to themselves. It doesn't matter if they don't know the whole speech – for this exercise the repetition of a few lines or one phrase is enough – the ownership of the language is key. You can use this exercise as a springboard to allow actors to bring their own interpretative qualities to a speech, and discover a relationship with the words that is entirely personal and intuitive.

## EXERCISE

The impulse to speak **https://vimeo.com/121689948**

Once everyone has been modelled, invite all the students into the space to take up their first positions. Ensure they all have room to move. This time make the handclaps yourself, allowing them a little time to embody the shapes in silence and, on your double handclap, to return to their starting shapes. On your command of 'Action', the students can come to life naturalistically and start to speak the speech quietly to themselves. It doesn't matter if they don't know all the words, they can simply repeat a few key phrases; the aim is to let the language emerge as a consequence of what is being felt in the body, allowing them the opportunity to explore their personal impulse to speak. You can move around the room allowing each student a turn to speak the words on their own.

## EXERCISE

### Prompting

Begin again with a sculptor and a model. The sculptor shapes the model, as before, and they move through the exercise of handclaps and initial movements. Now the sculptor takes on the role of prompter and the model becomes the actor. The responsibility for the words will lie with the prompter.

On your command of 'Action', the actor is released from her still image and moves naturalistically – it is really important that she does move, no matter how small her initial action – once moving she has free rein to explore her physicality. The prompter holds the script and, staying very close to the actor, begins to prompt the words in her ear, line by line. The words will already be familiar to both of them through the techniques and exercises in Part One. When the actor hears the words, she speaks them, using this exercise as an opportunity to explore her physicality and experience how it *feels* to say these words. Whether her instinct is to remain completely still or to pace around the room is of no significance, the key is that she owns her body, voice and thoughts for herself and speaks the words as naturally as possible.

> Meanwhile the prompter's role is exacting; every actor should experience this activity, it offers a steep acting learning curve. Prompting requires half whispering/half acting the words into the ear of the actor, loud enough for them to hear, but not overpowering them and with just enough intention of feeling. There will be inevitable hiccups of communication between the two and the flow of language will often be interrupted – this doesn't matter, as the exercise is designed to loosen up the actors.

Once the actors get the hang of the game they can become very excited at the idea of complete physical freedom and start to genuinely explore. I have seen actors and students run from one wall to another, roll up in a ball, plaster themselves flat to the floor or bang on the door to get out, meanwhile receiving the prompted lines and speaking them. None of these actions necessarily ends up in a final production, the games are designed to release an actor's creativity and allow them to truly own the language for themselves. The key to success within the exercise is that the prompter keeps up with the actor and ensures that the actor keeps speaking the lines. Later in rehearsal an actor may speak the same lines in complete stillness, but the memory of his explosive energetic actions will remain in his mind and innately inform his speaking.

Sometimes the exercise allows the actors to engage so intensely with the physical life of the character, the results can be transformative for actor, director and production. In 2005, I worked on *King Lear* with a group of hard-to-reach teenagers in Beckton, creating the *Beckton Lear*. One particular student somersaulted backward off a wall during this exercise, whilst we were exploring Edmund's 'bastard' speech:

EDMUND
Why bastard, wherefore base?

Why brand they us
With base, with baseness, bastardy, base, base?
*King Lear*, 1.2

Another student found an unimaginably small box and managed to squeeze himself into it, as Poor Tom:

EDGAR
That's something yet. Edgar I nothing am.
*King Lear*, 2.2

This boy had himself been a refugee in Somalia and his grasp of English was poor, but he connected with the persecution of Edgar more intensely than anyone I have ever worked with before or since. I kept both these physical expressions of character in the production, allowing the students a genuine ownership of language and character.

I have rehearsed entire productions of Shakespeare using this technique, using the actor's initial responses to the language to start to direct the scenes. Remarkably it doesn't take more time than a 'normal' rehearsal and, by needing to involve the company as prompters – everyone takes turns prompting each other and thereby gets to speak each other's parts – it is a sure way of building a true ensemble in the room.

# Exploding the mind's eye images

This is a game within in a game. It is, in one sense, an indulgence that can easily be missed out of a rehearsal process, but once you have played it, the power of the results is compelling enough to keep the game in your toolbox. It offers an excellent means of unlocking Shakespeare's language.

## EXERCISE

Using Hamlet's soliloquy, begin, as before, with a sculptor and a model, and allow them to move through the exercise of handclaps and initial movements. As before, the sculptor takes on the role of prompter and the model becomes the actor. On your command of 'Action', the model is released from his still image and moves naturalistically, meanwhile the prompter begins to prompt the actor with the lines. All this should be routine for the partners; the focus of the game is on the rest of the group who are watching. They are about to enter and embody the worlds of Hamlet's mind's eye.

The prompter begins and the actor moves and speaks:

O that this too too solid flesh would melt
Thaw and dissolve itself into a dew

The other actors watch and listen attentively; they are waiting to discover what Hamlet sees in his mind's eye. As soon as an actor sitting in the group hears a phrase that illuminates Hamlet's imagination, he stops the exercise – simply by saying, 'Stop', standing up and moving into the space. Hamlet stops speaking and he and the prompter wait in the circle. This new actor brings further actors from the group into the space with him (as many as he needs; three is a good maximum, he may only need one). He moulds them into a still picture of the image he has heard, thereby exploding Hamlet's mind's eye into three-dimensional space. In this speech, these first pictures are very likely to concentrate on abstract images of melting flesh. Without speaking, he should try to make the image as explicit and clear as he can; you can offer encouragement to help him do so if the images are too generalized to begin with.

Once the actor has created his particular mind's eye image for Hamlet, he goes through the exercise of bringing the image to life with handclaps and reversing them back to the beginning with a double handclap. Now the space has Hamlet, the prompter and the new models – frozen starting images depicting Hamlet's mind's eye.

On your command of 'Action', everyone in the acting space comes to life. The prompter begins once more from the beginning of the speech, Hamlet moves around the space, taking the prompts and speaking the lines and, at the same time, the images

themselves come to life – moving smoothly and repeating their
original actions. Hamlet cannot interact with these images – you
cannot interfere with the images in your mind's eye – but he should
be aware of them and let their physical and emotional quality affect
him in any way he sees fit.

The speech continues (you should encourage the prompter and
Hamlet to get to the end of each phrase):

Or that the Everlasting had not fix'd
His canon 'gainst self slaughter; O God, God!

Once more, actors in the main group will stop the exercise, bring
fellow actors into the acting space and create fresh mind's eye
images emanating from these next lines. More than one actor can
come into the space at the same time, as long as there are enough
people to create images. These images will be centred on God, the
Bible and forbidden suicide. (If no one in the group stops the action,
you should encourage them to do so – the imagery here is well
worth investigation. When actors are new to the game, they may
need encouragement to see that there are mind's eye pictures in
almost everything that is spoken.)

The key to success for this exercise is for the actors who are moulded
into mind's eye images to commit entirely to their role, however abstract
it may be and whatever it may entail. An interesting observation I have
made over the years is that, regardless of who plays this game, the
vast majority of images created are of a biblical or at the very least a
classical nature. That Shakespeare paints with words is a well worn
adage; when you take the time to explore the nature of the paintings,
it becomes clear that the job of the actor is to convey images of a
sublime, absolute and rare quality that naturally transcend everyday
existence. The exploration can begin with this exercise, which should
be as joyful, crazed and free from inhibition as it is possible to be.

You can stop and start the exercise as many times as you like. It's also very useful to do a version where the mind's eye images can make sound – albeit quietly – to increase the intensity of the created images in order to put more pressure on Hamlet.

Ensure that each stage is taken with care and attention to detail – the whole exercise is a fascinating luxury and although it would be indulgent to present its workings on stage, the more detailed and personal the images become, the more powerful the exercise reveals itself to be. Its exact purpose is for the actor to begin to understand the imaginative potency of the images in his mind's eye and the infinite possibilities of interpretation these images present. The exercise allows the whole group of actors to work together to explore and expand their understanding of the words and to find a common physical understanding of the language together.

As the game continues on through the speech, you will need to bring the actors back to their semi-circle in order to continue creating fresh mind's eye images. Do this as often as you need, depending on the size of the group you are working with. Encourage the actors to remember the images they have been given, so they can replicate them when you 'run' through the speech. You should also encourage the group to explore being both sculptor and model, as they get up to create mind's eye images, in order to stretch the different muscles that both techniques require. In this way you can work through the whole speech, phrase by phrase, discovering the different qualities of image that Hamlet sees.

Once you have played the exercise all the way through the speech, you can effectively 'run' it, with the prompter feeding the lines to Hamlet, whilst actors from the group enter the space to physically embody each of the mind's eye images they have invented. The images change when different lines are spoken, and as explored in Chapter 8, the list of mind's eye images in this speech is extensive. From Hamlet's world weariness:

How weary, stale, flat and unprofitable,
Seem to me all the uses of this world.

to his father, a devoted husband protecting his wife's cheek:

              so loving to my mother,
That he might not beteem the winds of heaven
Visit her face too roughly.

to the tears of Niobe:

   Like Niobe, all tears. Why she, even she

to an unthinking beast:

   O Heaven, a beast that wants discourse of reason
   Would have mourn'd longer

to the copulating couple in their incestuous sheets:

              O, most wicked speed, to post
   With such dexterity to incestuous sheets!

When the exercise has run its course, ask the actor to speak the speech on his own – he may well know most of the lines by now, but the prompter should stand by to prompt if needed. Encourage the actor to do a version of the speech that is physically still (but not physically locked) and to explore the kaleidoscopic nature of Hamlet's imagination, as the images created by the group come to life in his mind's eye as he speaks. Once more, Coleridge's serpent, twisting and untwisting its own strength, provides the perfect description of the language, as one image is not simply replaced by the next, but indeed created by the image that comes before it.

# Provocations

## Who do I see in my mind's eye?

Play the game with the exactly same format; prompter, Hamlet and a group of actors who will come in to create mind's eye images. This time the heart of the exercise is to concentrate solely on whom Hamlet sees in his mind's eye and what they are doing. This requires a good knowledge of the play and is really useful to play in later rehearsals. The purpose of the exercise is to provoke the actors to consider what the mind's eye does beyond the obvious – and suggest that we see people in our mind's eye even when we're not speaking about them.

The population of our close families pack our mind's eyes, whether we like it or not, and one of the great pleasures of performing Shakespeare is the chance to explore where the language brings these images to life and, furthermore, to keep these people alive in our mind's eye whilst acting. Hamlet makes many references to his mother, father and uncle during the speech and these are relatively easy to interpret, but does he see them at any other points in the speech? And if so, what are they doing? Are they in the past or the future? Is Hamlet there too? Furthermore does he see Ophelia and, if so, when? You could explore a version where she is the sole constant feature in his mind's eye throughout the speech. Is that tortuous or wonderful? How and when does it change?

A further provocation is to use the exercise solely to explore when and whether he sees himself in his mind's eye. And if so, is it himself in his past or in his future? I would suggest that we rarely see ourselves as we are in the 'here and now', but are beset by an infinite variety of images of ourselves from our past – from our short-term, middling or distant childhoods – and of our future lives, with fantastical, romantic or revengeful visions.

## The one and only image

Is there an overriding image in Hamlet's mind's eye right from the start, which he only puts into words later? For example: the copulating of his mother and uncle between incestuous sheets? Or the image of his mother's new shoes, which she wore as she followed his father's coffin, weeping copious tears. Very often one is plagued or haunted by one sole image and although one can speak of other things, there is one residing picture or impression, which the mind cannot shake. This goes hand-in-hand with speaking the language at the moment you think and feel it – although it often exists as an unnamed image or sensation before you find the words with which to express it.

Use the exercise to agree upon such an image; and allow the group to create and embody it as Hamlet speaks the speech. Encourage the actor to explore how much pressure this puts on him before he finally comes to describe it and the pained ecstasy it requires to bring the image into life with words. This exploration should encourage a renewed sensitivity towards speaking the language and towards the actor's relationship with the images, provoking the actor to genuinely experience how it feels to generate and express the character's feelings.

In the next chapter these games are expanded, and shared between characters within a scene.

# 11

# GAMES OF THE MIND'S EYE: SCENES

EXERCISES

- Chain of creativity
- Prompting
- Exploding the mind's eye images

## Sharing the mind's eye in a scene

Everything explored in Chapter 10 can be replicated with more than one actor on stage. Let's use a shortened section of Hamlet's scene with Ophelia.

HAMLET
I did love you once.
OPHELIA
Indeed, my lord, you made me believe so.
HAMLET
You should not have believed me;
I loved you not.
OPHELIA
I was the more deceived.
HAMLET
Get thee to a nunnery: why wouldst thou be a breeder of sinners?
I am myself indifferent honest; but yet I could accuse me of such

things that it were better my mother had not borne me: I am very proud, revengeful, ambitious, with more offences at my beck than I have thoughts to put them in, imagination to give them shape, or time to act them in. What should such fellows as I do crawling between earth and heaven? We are arrant knaves, all; believe none of us. Go thy ways to a nunnery. Where's your father?

OPHELIA

At home, my lord.

HAMLET

Let the doors be shut upon him, that he may play the fool no where but in's own house. Farewell.

*Hamlet*, 3.1

## EXERCISE

### Chain of creativity

Three actors play. One is the 'sculptor' and the other two the 'models' or the 'human clay'. The exercise is exactly the same as before, but now the sculptor has two starting images to create. Encourage the sculptor to keep the images apart and to investigate the distance and relationship between them. Once the sculptor has created two images she is happy with, she moves away from the models, who remain in the position, keeping as still as they can. The images now belong to the models and the chain of creativity can begin.

The sculptor now makes a series of slow handclaps in order to 'bring the models to life'. At each handclap, the models make one movement with their bodies, as if slowly moving forward in time and exploring how they may physically exist in relation to each other. Do they make eye contact? If Hamlet makes a move toward Ophelia, what is her physical response? And vice versa. As before, these movements are made not to attempt to *show* Hamlet and Ophelia to an audience, but rather to explore how it may *feel* to be in each other's presence.

After four or five handclaps, the sculptor makes a double handclap and the models reverse the movements they have made, in one smooth action, until they land back at their original pictures. Exploring this exercise in relation to another person – especially when their relationship is so highly charged – should have an almost animal-like effect on the actor; without language, it's vital that they read each other's bodies and begin to tune in to each other on a physical level.

## EXERCISE

### Prompting

This next stage is challenging for all three actors – especially the prompter, who must now move between the two actors, prompting them both and taking overall responsibility for the words. Begin as before with the prompter and two actors. On your command of 'Action', both actors are released from their still images and move naturalistically – as before, it is really important that both actors move. Encourage them to be very wary of making any casual physical contact – if either of them touches each other, it is essential that they explore the effects and allow these moments of touching to truly register.

The prompter holds the script and, moving between the two actors and staying very close to them to speak, he begins to prompt the words in their ears, line by line. At best, the prompter is akin to a lightning conductor of words, flying between the two characters and charging them with language. The actors hear the words and speak them, using this exercise as an opportunity to concentrate on the relationship with the other character, exploring their physical relationship and experiencing how it feels to **speak and listen** to each other. As before, the key is for the actors to own their bodies, voices and thoughts for themselves and speak the words as naturally as possible.

## EXERCISE

### Exploding the mind's eye images

Begin as before, with a sculptor and two models and allow them
to move through the exercise of handclaps and initial movements.
As before, the sculptor takes on the role of prompter and the
models become the actors. On your command of 'Action', the actors
are released from their still images and move naturalistically.
Meanwhile the prompter begins to move between them with the
lines. All this should be routine for the actors; the focus of the game
is on the rest of the group who are watching. They are about to
enter and embody the dual worlds of Hamlet's and Ophelia's minds'
eyes.

The prompter begins and the actors move and speak:

HAMLET
I did love you once.
OPHELIA
Indeed, my lord, you made me believe so.

Now the group waits to discover what both Hamlet and Ophelia
see in their two very different minds' eyes. As soon as an
actor sitting in the group hears a phrase that illuminates the
imagination of either character – or both – he stops the exercise,
as before, and brings in fellow actors to model the image. The
new actor must make it very clear whose inner life he is exploring
by creating his mind's eye image close to either Hamlet or
Ophelia.

This is a complex moment in the play and at some point in rehearsal a
number of inevitable questions will arise:

- Did they love each other?

- What was the nature of the relationship?

- How did he make her believe it?

This exercise should not be used to definitively answer these questions, but rather for the group to bring their own life experience and imagination to the room and begin to play with ideas. From these, an expansive and imaginative palette may be collectively created and potentially explored.

The exercise is time-consuming, but full of acting opportunity. The images created are likely to be in opposition with each other – Hamlet is unlikely to see what Ophelia sees – and for each line spoken there is minimum of two mind's eye images to begin with. You can judge for yourself how often to stop the exercise and explore the work so far. For example:

HAMLET
I did love you once.

- What does Hamlet see in his mind's eye as he speaks?

- What does Ophelia see in her mind's eye as she listens?

Are they the same images? Do we ever share the same mind's eye images with the people we speak to? Do we want to? Does it matter? Do we see what we want to see or what we don't want to see? Do we speak in order to make others see what we see?

The essential outcome of the exercise is to provoke the actors into asking these kinds of questions, thereby revealing the human mystery and infinite interpretation of the mind's eye. The power of seeing with the mind's eye (or the triple eye) is at the heart of Shakespeare's poetic invention; it will – and should – remain in some way unfathomable for us all. It is very good to have something larger and better than all of us at work in the rehearsal room.

It's also essential to push the exercise forward and encourage the group to continue creating images, in the knowledge that there will be no definitive version. It may well be that, at the end of the short section, the two actors playing Hamlet and Ophelia express very strong feelings about what they are seeing. If this is the case, play the game again, using two new actors to play the roles and allowing the two original actors to create and explore the mind's eye images.

# Provocations

The same provocations apply whether you are exploring a soliloquy, an intimate scene between two lovers or indeed a huge court scene.

## Who do I see in my mind's eye?

Perhaps Hamlet cannot shake the sight of his mother from his mind's eye during the scene; it is a palpable reading of the play that his disgust at his mother's sexuality pushes him into rejecting Ophelia and specifically demanding that she gets to a nunnery – a place where no sexual act can exist. An obsession with his mother lends a potency to his words:

> HAMLET
> Get thee to a nunnery: why wouldst thou be a breeder of sinners?

Equally Hamlet may not be able to shake the image of his father's ghost from his mind's eye and furthermore, perhaps Ophelia cannot shake the sight of her own father from her mind's eye – he is after all a few feet away, listening to everything that is being said. Following this train of exploration, the group can use the exercise to create images of Gertrude, the Ghost and Polonius, alive and present in the space, as Hamlet and Ophelia try to communicate with each other. This would seem to be a potent line of exploration, with obvious psychological benefits for the actors to experience.

I would suggest that Shakespeare explores how Hamlet and Ophelia *share* a mind's eye image of Polonius in these next lines:

> HAMLET
> Where's your father?
> OPHELIA

At home, my lord.
HAMLET
Let the doors be shut upon him, that he may play the fool no where
but in's own house. Farewell.

It's likely that Hamlet is testing Ophelia and knows full well that Polonius
is listening, making her lie all the more painful. He knows she is lying
and perhaps she knows he knows. This is all the more painful if the
only mind's eye image they share during the whole scene is Ophelia's
spying father.

## The one and only image

Use the exercise as above to further explore the idea of one overriding
image that the character already has in their mind. This line of Hamlet's
would be an excellent one to explore and embody.

HAMLET
What should such fellows as I do crawling between earth and heaven?

The image of man crawling like a low animal, stuck between heaven
and earth, can be physically expressed by the group and palpably felt
by Hamlet, as he continues to speak to Ophelia. The intensity of the
image should rise, the closer Hamlet comes to speaking the lines, so
that the coining of the phrase itself is felt to be inevitable and completely
personal to him.

Furthermore you can reverse the exercise and explore what happens
when a character hears something that creates an image which gets
stuck in her mind's eye. For example, Ophelia has to hear these words
of rejection from Hamlet:

HAMLET
You should not have believed me;
I loved you not.

I would suggest that whatever image she sees in her mind's eye at
this time – whether it is a fantastical image of their happiness that runs

counter to his words, or a genuine image from a memory of their past love, or a picture of herself as a spinster in the future – gets stuck in her head and, just as she can't shake these words, neither can she shake this image. The group can explore and embody the image and Ophelia can actively use it to fight against, whilst she keeps attempting to communicate with Hamlet. This will give her the experience of having a *divided self,* a phrase used by Claudius to describe Ophelia later in the play.

Before leaving this luxurious work, ensure that the actors have the opportunity to play the scene alone – with only the prompter for help. The experience of knowing when they share an image and when they have diametrically opposing images is very useful and can create islands of loneliness between the characters. Encourage the actors to genuinely remember the sensations, pictures and emotions generated by the liveliness of the human images and to encase them all into their skulls to use when they are speaking the words alone.

# 12
# REHEARSAL TECHNIQUES

EXERCISES

- Circle of applause
- Shadow-boxing

## Soliloquy

Too often in the rehearsal process the focus is on the person speaking and not on the person – or people – listening, which can result in one actor speaking for what seems like an eternity whilst everyone stands around, usually very still, waiting for their turn. In Chapter 9 I introduced the idea of **active listening**; the actor listening must have an *active need* to hear the words that are being spoken, whilst the actor speaking must have an *active need* to be heard. This *mutual need* to speak and listen is essential for Shakespeare's language to be alive on stage. Equally an actor speaking a soliloquy must *need* to speak and learn how to tune into whether the audience is listening.

Shakespeare's blank verse can be likened to the waves of the sea – they have a momentum all of their own and *will* come crashing down onto the beach, no matter what you do to stop them. Tuning into the audience is akin to riding the waves of verse.

To begin we'll use Caliban's soliloquy, which we looked at in Chapter 4:

CALIBAN
All the infections that the sun sucks up

From bogs, fens, flats, on Prosper fall and make him
By inchmeal a disease! His spirits hear me
And yet I needs must curse. But they'll nor pinch,
Fright me with urchin-shows, pitch me i' th' mire,
Nor lead me like a firebrand in the dark
Out of my way, unless he bid 'em. But
For every trifle are they set upon me,
Sometime like apes that mow and chatter at me,
And after bite me, then like hedgehogs which
Lie tumbling in my barefoot way and mount
Their pricks at my footfall. Sometime am I
All wound with adders who with cloven tongues
Do hiss me into madness. Lo, now, lo!
Here comes a spirit of his, and to torment me
For bringing wood in slowly. I'll fall flat.
Perchance he will not mind me.
*The Tempest*, 2.2

## EXERCISE

### Circle of applause

One actor sits or stands in the space to play Caliban. The rest of the
group sits around him in the semi-circle. The actor should know the
speech, or at least have a really good knowledge of it, so he doesn't
rely wholly on the script. The actors sitting around the circle close
their eyes and prepare to listen. 'Caliban' begins to speak.

The actors sitting in the circle are going to **feed back** when
they hear a phrase that engages their curiosity and also when they
hear the conclusion of a phrase. Specifically there are two types of
feedback the actors can give. The first is 'encouragement'; this is
given at the end of lines that have not concluded their sense, it can
be phrased as: '*yes?*', '*uh-uh?*', '*go on*', '*what else*', '*and ...?*'. The
second type of feedback is a ripple of applause, no more than a few
seconds, which can *only* be used when an actor has concluded the

sense of a phrase. The group can also add in '*bravo*'s and '*hurray*'s or some such words – their mood should be playful, quick-witted and quiet. In this way 'Caliban' begins to learn where and when the sense of the speech lands with an audience. *He should not wait or pause for their interjections, but rather ride them like waves when they come.* The experience of the exercise teaches, and hopefully confirms for him, how and where the thread of sense runs through a speech.

I once played this game with a group of students who instinctively turned it into a kind of gospel meeting – whooping with delight when they collectively understood a phrase and then immediately returning to a hushed 'sacred' silence with which to listen more. The actor speaking became extremely enthused and began repeating certain phrases that were 'going down well' in order to receive more love from her 'blind' audience. It was immensely pleasurable for everyone and the actor said later that, whenever she performed the speech in the production, she kept the 'army of love and praise' she had received that day in her sense memory – it gave her a 'secret cushion of confidence'.

Played perfectly, the first four lines would run like this:

| CALIBAN | AUDIENCE |
|---|---|
| All the infections that the sun sucks up | *uh-uh?* |
| From bogs, fens, flats, on Prosper fall and make him | *yes?* |
| By inchmeal a disease! | applause |
| His spirits hear me | *and?* |
| And yet I needs must curse. | applause |
| But they'll nor pinch, | *yes?* |

The moments of applause mark where the audience's attention has landed and serves to re-energize the actor to continue; in this way the solitary experience of speaking a soliloquy becomes more like 'riding waves of applause'. Of course, in performance these 'waves of applause' are silent (it is unlikely that a modern-day audience will burst into spontaneous applause in the middle of a speech, although that does depend on where you may be performing), but if the actor has them in his head through playing this game, he knows when to expect to make the connection with the audience. In performance, if you get it right, you can feel the listening energy in the audience generated by the structure of the language.

This exercise is especially valuable for the actor to experience how quickly the audience will follow the speed and energy of his turns of thought in the middle of the changing lines. To recap, a **changing line** is when the first half of the line is the end of the previous thought and the second half is the beginning of the next thought, but it is as yet unfinished.

The first changing line in this speech is:

By inchmeal a disease! His spirits hear me

And as we have seen in this exercise, the connections land twice with the audience:

| By inchmeal a disease! | applause |
| His spirits hear me | *and*? |

There are always two potential connections with an audience within one changing line. The first will be applause and the second will be encouragement. This exercise teaches the actor that he can guide an audience through the most complicated of phrases by knowing whether they need more information from him at the end of a line or whether he has conclusively ended a phrase.

We looked at this next phrase in Chapter 4; playing this game, the phrase would read like this.

| CALIBAN | AUDIENCE |
| But they'll nor pinch, | *uh-uh?* |
| Fright me with urchin-shows, pitch me i' th' mire, | *uh-uh?* |
| Nor lead me like a firebrand in the dark | *uh-uh?* |
| Out of my way, unless he bid 'em. | applause |
| But | *yes!?* |

The space around the little word at the end and the fast dynamic energy it creates between the applause and the encouragement allows

Caliban to make a powerful and playful connection with the audience. Here, as always, the technique is universal, his interpretation will be unique.

Using this same exercise with a speech from *King John* reveals the structural difference between the early and late plays, thereby creating a completely different relationship between actor and audience. There are no changing lines in Constance's speech and therefore no energetic waves of applause on which to ride; but instead there are longer drives of encouragement, punctuated by applause, which pushes her inexorably forward.

| CONSTANCE | AUDIENCE |
|---|---|
| Grief fills the room up of my absent child, | *yes?* |
| Lies in his bed, walks up and down with me, | *yes?* |
| Puts on his pretty looks, repeats his words, | *uh-uh?* |
| Remembers me of all his gracious parts, | *yes?* |
| Stuffs out his vacant garments with his form; | *yes?* |
| Then, have I reason to be fond of grief? | applause |
| Fare you well: had you such a loss as I, | *yes* |
| I could give better comfort than you do. | applause |
| *King John*, 3.4 | |

Note the verbs as **heart attacks**, the poetic assembly of **last words**, the placing of the word **all**, and the keyword **reason** in the centre of the phrase.

# Provocations

## Pardon?

Add a third option for the group to use as feedback – the 'pardon'. If one of the actors listening in the group doesn't fully understand the sense of a phrase he can say, '*pardon?*' The actor must immediately repeat the phrase, trying as hard as he can to make himself understood until he gets either encouragement or applause. This can prove an essential means of showing the actor where the tricky parts of the speech are and where it requires care and attention to keep the audience with him. At best these 'pardons' will be collectively given from the group and it will be clear where the speech is difficult to understand. They usually occur when the actor isn't making it clear that there is more to say and actually needs more encouragement before he reaches the conclusion of a phrase.

Add in the option of 'playful booing' in addition to the 'pardon'. This exercise is not critical or made in judgement of the actor; the motivation behind it can be paraphrased as such: *'We don't understand and we want to understand, say it again and help us understand'*. The game explores an audience's 'blind' desire to hear debate and philosophy, not to criticize the actors. The group must maintain the 'blindness' as a disciplined part of the exercise. Ensure that all the actors take a turn in the middle and experience the playful booing as well as the encouragement and praise.

## Blinded

Play a completely blind version where the actor also closes his eyes, heightening everyone's concentrated listening in the room.

## EXERCISE

### Shadow-boxing [https://vimeo.com/121689949]

This exercise deepens the actor's physical and sensory response to the language and develops a physical ownership of the words. To begin, choose a soliloquy to work on as a group and play the game directly after a session working on the text, so that the words are fresh in the actors' minds. Everyone stands together in a circle and two actors come into the space to begin. They play as boxing partners, standing a few feet apart, so as *never* to make physical contact. They begin to shadow-box, throwing and receiving punches, using the full physicality of their bodies, *as if* they are truly engaged in a boxing match. They use the whole available space within the circle, maintaining eye contact and reading each other's bodies. Once they are physically engaged in the exercise, they begin to speak the text. This is also an extremely useful exercise for two actors to play together, when rehearsing scenes.

Allow the students to try just a few lines at first, so they get used to speaking the words and boxing at the same time. Encourage the natural instinct to 'throw' punches when speaking and 'receive' punches when listening. The actors around the circle become a 'prompting circle', so that the responsibility for remembering the words belongs to them and they feed in the lines if the 'boxers' need help. This allows the boxers to concentrate solely on boxing, whether speaking or listening. The boxers should never ask for a prompt, it should come naturally from the group. With a big enough group someone should know the next line!

After the boxing has been demonstrated and understood, split the whole group into partners and let everyone try the exercise around the room, shadow-boxing and speaking the lines of the soliloquy at the same time. Encourage the actors to feel the physical difference between 'throwing' the punches whilst speaking the lines and 'receiving' the punches whilst listening to the lines. It will be noisy in the room and should feel explosive and fun. Do make sure that players keep their distance from each other.

The exercise is not about throwing a punch on every word nor is it about throwing punches on every strong heartbeat; at best there should be a physical looseness in the boxer, who every so often throws a punch, thereby taking his partner completely by surprise. The exercise should produce instinctive freedom and a sense of danger between the two players. After a few minutes, gather everyone back to the large prompting circle and proceed to let each set of partners take a turn, reminding those on the outside to prompt if necessary.

The first round is played as practised, the speaker delivering the lines and throwing the punches whilst the listener receives the blows. The second round introduces the opposite way of playing; the speaker receives the punches whilst the listener delivers them. This is much harder and provides the learning curve of the exercise. How does it feel to deliver the punches, 'be on the front foot', whilst speaking and conversely how does it then feel to be receiving punches, 'be on the back foot', whilst speaking. Meanwhile, how does it feel to receive punches whilst listening and lastly how does it feel to throw punches whilst listening? And what is the difference between the two experiences? There is no single or simple answer to this question, nor is there a right or wrong way to play – both ways are valid.

Speaking whilst receiving the punches offers a more subtle experience and is perhaps more akin to acting on stage, where you are sensitive to everything around you, not only from your fellow actors, but from the audience, the atmosphere and from your own imagination, which may beset you with all kinds of images and thoughts at any time. Meanwhile, listening to the words whilst throwing punches may seem initially to be counter-intuitive, but having played Goneril for an eighteen-month run and having to receive and absorb the almighty curse of sterility into my womb on a nightly basis, I can confirm that I was often overwhelmed by the instinct to deal King Lear an almighty blow. The exercise turns listening into receiving, and by physically receiving the language the actor may be more likely to explore – emotionally and intellectually – how they are thereby changed by it.

The final stage of the exercise is for the actors to maintain the threat of the throwing and receiving in their bodies *without ever boxing*, all that remains is that they *might* at some point throw or receive a punch. The boxers begin as before, fully committing to the physical exercises, but with each repeat of the scene, they decrease the amount of outward physical energy and focus on the threat and possibility of what they may do. Encourage them to do this very gradually, so that the exercise leaves them with an internal 'bounce' and the very strong likelihood that the physicality could burst out of them at any moment. Except it never actually does.

## Provocation

The shadow-boxing works really well for an actor working on a soliloquy. His sparring partner should generously allow the time for him to practise throwing and receiving punches, gradually decreasing the outward physical energy, and leaving him with an inner physical life which bubbles away with a potential danger that may burst through, but never does. I am not suggesting that every actor should resemble a boxer, but the remnants of the exercise can prove very useful in releasing an actor from feeling physically locked and placing the words 'in the body'.

# 13
# RUN-THROUGHS

Actors and students should love run-throughs, but very often they freeze in panic and fear while creativity flies out of the window. I have developed these different ways of working through the play, just at the moment they are ready to start running. Essentially these run-throughs require no interruption from me; their purpose is to generate a love and pleasure within the actors' experience and to empower them to develop ownership of the whole production not just their part.

## This is the part

At regular intervals throughout rehearsal, make a run-through of what you have rehearsed so far. Ensure that you have (more than once) achieved what you want from a collection of scenes and the actors have (more than once) begun to explore their intellectual and emotional engagement with rigour and discipline. This run-through provides a relief from that concentrated work and involves the whole cast, who should have been in rehearsal as much as possible. The purpose is to try and run the scenes as rehearsed, but not to stop when something goes amiss. The only rule is that they must, as an ensemble, keep the story going.

Before this run-through, remind them it is a rehearsal and not a performance and that they will learn about themselves, their part and the whole show through this exercise. Begin the run-through; no scripts anywhere to be seen. If and when an actor forgets his words he simply says, 'This is the part ...' and continues by describing what it is he does or says or feels in that particular part of the play, using his own words. If he then remembers the text, he can return to it, or his fellow actor can join in, either returning to Shakespeare's language or describing what he does in the scene. It should and will be chaotic and pleasurable, as long as the pressure to achieve perfection is absent and there is no judgement from you as director.

Anything goes, as long as everyone is trying to remember what they have rehearsed and creating the atmosphere generated by the rehearsals, but not panicking when they can't. The cast (and you) will very quickly learn where the tricky spots are within the scenes and be more prepared to rehearse them next time.

Keep repeating this exercise throughout the rehearsal period; if all goes well there will be fewer moments of falling into, 'This is the part …' each time you do it.

# Gibberish run-through

Towards the end of rehearsal, when the cast are very much ready to put everything together, make an entire run-through of the play with everyone speaking gibberish. Allow them to practise for a little while first, testing out and discovering how their own gibberish language will sound. The real discoveries will be made through how specifically communicative the actor can be, using the rhythm of the language without using words. Crucially the gibberish must be specific to the rhythm of the line. It cannot be a mess. If the line is:

All the infections that the sun sucks up

the gibberish version cannot sound like this:

blah dee blah blah blah blah blah ble sta fla

as this has no rhythmic resemblance to the line. The rhythm of the gibberish version (whatever sound the actor makes) must be the same as the line. So the gibberish version could go like this:

blah dee blahblahblah blah blah ble sta fla

The sound doesn't matter; the rhythm is essential.

The real challenge of the gibberish run-through is for the actors with long speeches; they must make every line specific and not resort to generalizing, meanwhile those receiving the language must attempt to know where they are at every point in the speech. Some interesting discoveries will always be made. It's fascinating how every actor creates their own particular way of making gibberish.

You may well want to use the gibberish technique to rehearse scenes, but don't try it too early; it is an exercise that works when an actor really owns the language; if you do it too soon, it will be difficult and prove really disheartening.

# The singing run-through

The same as above, but instead of gibberish, the actors must sing their way through the play. This run-through uses the specific cathartic quality of music to allow the emotional highs and lows of the production to flourish at extreme levels. Singing ability is not necessary for success in this exercise – but imagination is. The actors should not be after a constant 'recitative' style, where they simply make some singing notes as they speak, but rather you can encourage them to explore what musical mode their character embodies. Give them the opportunity to mix up the musical idioms: jazz, swing, blues, opera, rock, heavy metal, pop, folk, country; the list should be long and all can be embodied within the panorama of a Shakespeare play.

This is not an exercise in style; at best it can create a chaotic clash of high emotion. My favourite example of this game was during a rehearsal of *Cymbeline*, in the scene when Cloten rows with Imogen. She affected high opera and he was an Elvis impersonator; neither would back down from their idiom – a great example of never picking up each other's tone – and the scene exploded into the room in a way that it had never done before.

Again, you may well want to use the singing technique to rehearse scenes, but don't try it too early or too often. One singing run-through is normally enough.

# Playing each other's parts

Run through the play with this instruction to the actors: 'You can play any part except your own and as an ensemble you must keep the show going.' Begin each scene with the characters who are present on stage, but swap them so they have to play their opposite part. For example, the opening scene to *King Lear* begins with Kent speaking to Gloucester; this run-through would begin with Kent speaking Gloucester's lines and Gloucester speaking Kent's lines. It's a fantastic test as to whether an actor knows what is said to him or whether he just waits for his cue. Some paraphrasing will inevitably occur in this run-through, but for the most part the actors should try to say each other's lines and play opposite each other in key scenes to feel what it's like to receive the language that they normally speak.

If an actor wants to take over a particular part in a particular scene, he gives the existing player a few lines and then simply tags him on the shoulder to have a turn. There can often be a queue of actors waiting to tag each other to 'have a go' at certain parts. Unlike the previous two run-throughs, this one can require some intervention from the director. Sometimes there is an over-enthusiastic actor who – Bottom-like – wants to play every single part in the play. I have a distinct memory of a student in a production of *King Lear* who had never learnt his own lines and whose laziness was driving me to distraction in rehearsal, but who leapt upon this game with over-excited fervour, attempting to play every part and dominate the proceedings. He was admonished!

This is not an opportunity to impersonate the other actors, nor is it an opportunity to do a part 'better'. The key to this run-through is for the actors to understand what the production feels like inside a scene, but outside of their own constructed world. For example, this run-through is a revelation for an actor playing Rosalind, when she experiences what it's like for Orlando and Celia to listen to her. It's a revelation for an actor playing Imogen in *Cymbeline* to get the chance to emerge from the trunk, whilst the actor normally playing Iachimo lies trembling in bed. It's a revelation for the actor playing Caliban to torture the actor who normally plays Prospero.

The success of this run-through is wholly dependent on the actors' commitment to their part throughout the rehearsal period, starting on day one, with a detailed analysis of exactly what they say – line by line. They are not called run-throughs for nothing; you can't run before you can walk.

# The park

I have directed productions of *The Tempest*, *King Lear*, *A Midsummer Night's Dream* and *Cymbeline* with students from the USA at BADA and a production of *Twelfth Night* with British drama students at RADA. All these productions have one thing in common; they have all had an unofficial run-through in Regents Park, London. Each one has been a seismic experience and revealed the life force within Shakespeare's plays with fresh surprises. I recommend taking your actors to a park or an open space, as close as possible in time to your public perfor- mances and giving them this instruction: 'This open space is your set, play the play.'

Personally, these run-throughs will stay with me forever, specifically as proof that the discipline and rigour of a rehearsal period can result in a freedom and liberty which becomes unforgettable for everyone involved. Ariel hung upside down from a tree, Caliban wrestled semi- naked in the muddy leaves – we began *The Tempest* run-through in a thunder storm. Edgar was also bare, in mud and leaves, and cut a lonesome figure *running* for his life. The instinct to run was a constant theme through every play; given the chance, the actors wanted to run fast, sometimes to find a place for their scene to be played and sometimes to experience exactly what their character needed, whether it was running for their lives or running towards the one they loved – many more people run in these plays than perhaps we realize.

Antonio and Sebastian sat on a park bench in *Twelfth Night*, almost unable to tear themselves away from each other – looking out to the distant horizon. Having a horizon to look towards affected their sight and deepened their relationship to nature and fortune. As for Belarius, Arviragus and Guiderius, they disappeared into the bushes to make themselves a home when we began the run-through of *Cymbeline*, only to re-appear – deeply scratched by thorns and branches – with a joyful ecstasy of nature that I could have only dreamed of. Imogen climbed onto an ornate and complicated marble statue adorned with mini waterfalls to make herself her bed. And when Viola heard the name Sebastian and hoped it was her brother, the words, 'Prove true, imagination, O, prove true' (*Twelfth Night*, 3.4), had a resonance that stopped us all in our tracks. I didn't tell any of the actors to do any of these things.

Once you've tried as many of these games, exercises and techniques as you like and you have a production ready to perform, please go to a park, take no costumes or props and let the actors own the play.

**To share the final thoughts of drama students, see: [https://vimeo.com/121689953]**

# EXERCISE VIDEOS

To view a particular video, please visit its URL below, or go to: https://vimeo.com/channels/crackingshakespeare

# INDEX